S0-BEA-382

PAST MASTERS

PAST MASTERS

AND OTHER PAPERS

THOMAS MANN

Translated by H. T. Lowe-Porter

Essay Index Reprint Series

Originally published by:
MARTIN SECKER

BOOKS FOR LIBRARIES PRESS
FREEPORT, NEW YORK

First Published 1933
Reprinted 1968

Reprinted from a copy in the collections of
The Brooklyn Public Library

LIBRARY OF CONGRESS CATALOG CARD NUMBER:
68-25605

PRINTED IN THE UNITED STATES OF AMERICA

FOREWORD

The introductory essay in this volume, "Richard Wagner, his Sufferings and Greatness," appeared in the April number of the Neue Rundschau *of this year, being Thomas Mann's contribution to the celebrations attending the fiftieth anniversary of the composer's death. The second essay, "Goethe, Novelist," was published as epilogue to the Epicon edition of the* ELECTIVE AFFINITIES *and is here included as a late but not less vital and unique tribute to the Goethe anniversary of 1932. The remaining eleven essays have been chosen by Dr. Mann from the three volumes which appeared in Germany under the titles* REDE UND ANTWORT (1922), BEMÜHUNGEN (1925) *and* DIE FORDERUNG DES TAGES (1930). *These volumes contain essays, speeches, book reviews and occasional addresses written or delivered by Dr. Mann over a period of some twenty-five years of his creative, literary and public activity.*

In presenting these papers to English readers, it has not been thought necessary or desirable to deprive them of their "occasional" form or flavour. Filing down and polishing in order to make a volume of collected papers present a unified or literary effect is more usual with English than with German authors; thus the present collection may lay itself open to the charge of being more heterogeneous and casual, less literary than we might expect from an author whose high repute among us is almost altogether that of a great novelist, story-teller and master of style. But the risk is incurred, for the positive gain of offering to English-speaking readers—never more pertinently or pregnantly than now—this view of a German author who is not less eminently "Schriftsteller" *than* "Dichter," *to employ the antithesis habitual to his own thought: no more creative artist than writer, man of letters, even publicist. But as he himself has said more than once, "the distinction between the two does not run outwardly, between the products, but inwardly, within the personality, and even there is entirely fluid"; and no one who reads the present volume can fail to realise its organic unity with the novels or to recognise the same creative and critical philosophy to which he has given thematic treatment in his imaginative works. One fancies future students, rejoicing in the copious material afforded by the essays and speeches, playing the fascinating game of marking down the author's literary method and tracing the development of the creative idea through the indications present in the critical product. For instance, in several essays in this volume one thinks to find some of the "mythical-psychological" preoccupations of the forthcoming long novel* JOSEPH AND HIS BRETHREN. *Among English authors a similar method is pursued by Aldous Huxley.*

FOREWORD

To quote Dr. Mann himself: "My essay-writing proclivities seem fated to accompany or to act as critique upon my more creative work"; "the painful and conscientious searchings exhibited in THE REFLECTIONS OF A NON-POLITICAL MAN, *by dint of which the worst of the introspective burden was lifted from the novel"* (i.e. THE MAGIC MOUNTAIN); *"work on* THE MAGIC MOUNTAIN *was accompanied by the composition of critical essays . . . which were its immediate prose offshoot"; and finally, "what he is working on is never merely the task in hand, for everything else is weighing upon him and burdening the productive moment." The last quotation is from the first essay in this volume, and it refers to Wagner's method of work; but might equally well have been written about the author himself. The truth is, that the organic nature of creation is a destiny—sometimes a nemesis—to the creator; and the quotation is applicable not merely to the technique of composition. For that technique must have inward harmony with what is in fact the source of Thomas Mann's special creative impulse and vitality: I mean his extraordinary power of co-ordinating his vision into all four points of time's compass—past and future, present and eternity. In this volume we shall escape few or none of the resultant antinomies of his habitual thought; yet be stimulated—as when we read the imaginative works—by the sense that we are rising far enough above them to get glimpses, as though from a great height, of their returning arcs.*

In the essay on Lessing Dr. Mann says: "The

view that the poet must not be a controversialist is deep-rooted in the German mind. He is supposed to accept all phenomena as they come, with calm and lofty simplicity, and then transmute them. He is degraded and dishonoured if he display any feeling about the times or the world he lives in, any sensitiveness towards its bad or base or stupid manifestations. He is descending into the market-place, he is 'mixing in trade.'" Controversialist in the sense that Lessing was, Thomas Mann can hardly be considered; but the present volume—as also the circumstances under which it is appearing—makes it clear that in him the cultural and political elements lie mingled, and that he accepts not only the fact but its national implications as well. The essay on Freud, written some five years ago, offers a widely and deeply based criticism of the most modern political trends; while the one called "Culture and Socialism," containing the author's apologia for his own politico-cultural evolution, is at the same time less personal than national in its analysis. Indeed, hardly any of these essays escapes being in some sense an epitome of the spiritual and intellectual evolution of the author's nation. Though how far his own transcends theirs is illuminated by the following passage from the same essay: "Whereas originally the intellectual, in the shape of individualistic idealism, was bound up with the conception of culture, while the social concept, the class idea, never denied its purely economic origins, it is in these days the latter that entertains toward the things of the mind far friendlier feelings than do its folk- and middle-class opponents, whose conservatism has almost lost touch with the living spirit and its patent claims. I have . . . referred to the morbid and dangerous state of tension which has been set up in the world between mind, the height which the peak of humanity has already reached and made its own, and actual reality, and the state of enlightenment thought to be possible and attainable therein. It is the workers who display an undoubtedly stronger and more vital will toward the relaxing of this humiliating and dangerous tension than do their cultural opponents." To what extent, however, we should guard against a too narrowly political interpretation of this paragraph, can be seen from the close of the essay, where the whimsical yet serious suggestion is made that "Karl Marx read Friedrich Hölderlin." Here the poet in Dr. Mann triumphs over the "writer" and speaks again in the accents of the artist, whose mission it is to reconcile form and matter.

H. T. L.-P.

CONTENTS

THE SUFFERINGS AND GREATNESS OF RICHARD WAGNER

THE SUFFERINGS AND GREATNESS OF RICHARD WAGNER

Il y a là mes blâmes, mes éloges et tout ce que j'ai dit.
MAURICE BARRÈS.

SUFFERING and great as that nineteenth century whose complete expression he is, the mental image of Richard Wagner stands before my eyes. Scored through and through with all his century's unmistakable traits, surcharged with all its driving forces, so I see his image; and scarcely can I distinguish between my two loves: love of his work, as magnificently equivocal, suspect and compelling a phenomenon as any in the world of art, and love of the century during most of which he lived his restless, harassed, tormented, possessed, miscomprehended life. We of to-day, absorbed as we are in tasks which—for novelty and difficulty at least—never saw their like, we have no time and little wish to give its due to the epoch—we call it the bourgeois—now dropping away behind us. Our attitude toward the nineteenth century is that of sons toward a father: critical, as is only fair. We shrug our shoulders alike over its belief—which was a belief in ideas—

and over its unbelief, that is to say, its melancholy relativism. Its attachment to liberal ideas of reason and progress seems to us laughable, its materialism all too crass, its monistic solution of the riddle of the universe full of shallow complacency. And yet its scientific self-sufficiency is atoned for, yes, outweighed, by the pessimism, the musical bond with night and death, which will very likely one day seem its strongest trait. Though another, not unconnected with it, is its wilful love of mere largeness, its taste for the monumental and standard, the copious and grandiose—this again, strange to say, coupled with an infatuation for the very small and the circumstantial, for the minutiæ of mental processes. Yes, greatness, of a turbid, suffering kind; disillusioned, yet bitterly, fanatically aware of truth; conscious too of the brief, incredulous bliss to be snatched from beauty as she flies—such greatness as this was the meaning and mark of the nineteenth century. Plastically represented it would resemble a Michaelangelo statue, an Atlas of the moral world, stretching and relaxing his muscles. Giant burdens were borne in that day—epic burdens, in the full sense of that strong word: one thinks not only of Balzac and Tolstoi, one thinks of Wagner himself. When the latter, in 1851, sent his friend Liszt a letter with the formal plan of the *Ring*, Liszt answered from Weimar: "Go on with it, and work on regardless! You ought to take for your motto the one the Chapter of the Cathedral of Seville gave to the architect who built it: 'Build us,' they said, 'such a temple that future generations will say the Chapter was mad to undertake anything so extraordinary.' And yet—there stands the Cathedral." That is genuine nineteenth century.

The enchanted garden of French impressionistic painting, the English, French and Russian novel, German science, German music—no, it was not such a bad age, in fact it was a perfect forest of giants. And only now, looking back from a distance, are we able to see the family likeness among them all, the stamp which, in all their manifold greatness, their age set upon them. Zola and Wagner, the *Rougon-Macquarts* and the *Ring of the Nibelungs*—fifty years ago who would have thought of putting them together? Yet they belong together. The kinship of spirit, aims and methods is most striking. It is not only the love of size, the propensity to the grandiose and the lavish; not only, in the sphere of technique, the Homeric leit-motif that they have in common. More than anything else it is a naturalism that amounts to the symbolic and the mythical. Who can fail to see in Zola's epic the tendency to symbol and myth that gives his characters their over-life-size air? That Second Empire Astarte, Nana, is she not symbol and myth? Where does she get her name? It sounds like the babbling of primitive man. Nana was a cognomen of the Babylonian Ishtar: did Zola know that? So much the more remarkable and significant, if he did not.

Tolstoi too has the same naturalistic magnificence of scale, the same democratic amplitude. He too has the leit-motif, the self-quotation, the standing phrases to describe his characters. He has often been criticised for his relentless carrying through, his refusal to indulge his reader, his deliberate and splendid longwindedness. And of Wagner Nietzsche says that he is surely the impolitest of all geniuses : he takes his hearer as it were—as though—he keeps on saying a thing until in desperation one believes it. Here they are alike ; but more profoundly so in their common possession of social and ethical elements. Wagner saw in art a sacred arcanum, a means of salvation for a corrupted society, whereas Tolstoi, toward the end of his life, repudiated it altogether, as trivial and self-indulgent ; but this disparity is not important. For as self-indulgence Wagner too repudiated art. He wanted it saved and purified for the sake of a corrupted society. He was all for catharsis and purification, he dreamed of an æsthetic consecration which should cleanse society of luxury, the greed of gold and all unloveliness ; hence his social ethics were closely akin to those of the Russian epic writer. And there is a likeness in their destinies too ; for critics have seen in the character of both a temperamental split, causing something like a moral collapse, whereas the truth is, that both lives display throughout their course the strictest unity and consistency. It has seemed to people that Tolstoi, in his old age, fell into a kind of religious madness. They do not see that th Tolstoi of the last period lay implicit in characters like Pierre Besuchov in *War and Peace* and Levin in *Anna Karenina.* Similarly, Nietzsche would have it that Wagner toward the end was a broken man, prostrate at the foot of the Cross ; he passes over the fact that the emotional atmosphere of *Tannhäuser* anticipates that of *Parsifal*, and that the latter is the final, splendidly logical summing-up of a life-work at bottom romantic and Christian in its spirit. Wagner's last work is also his most theatrical—and it would be hard to find an artist career more consistent than his. An art of essential sensuousness, based on symbolic formulas—for the leit-motif is a formula, nay, it is a monstrance, it claims an almost religious authority—must be leading back to the church celebration ; and indeed I do believe that the secret longing and ultimate ambition of all theatre is to return to the bosom of the ritual out of which—in both the pagan and the Christian world—it sprang. The art of the theatre is already baroque, it is Catholicism, it is the Church ; and an artist like Wagner, used to dealing with symbols and elevating monstrances, must have ended by feeling like a brother of priests, like a priest himself.

I have often thought about the likeness between Wagner and Ibsen, and found it hard to decide how much of it is due to their contemporaneity and how much to personal traits. For I could not but recognise, in the dialogue of Ibsen's bourgeois drama, means and effects, fascinations and wiles already known to me from the sound-world of the other artist; could not but be convinced of a kinship which in part of course lay in their common possession of genius, but how very much too in their way of being great! How much they are alike in their tremendous self-sufficiency, in the three-dimensional rotundity and consummateness of the life-work of both; social-revolutionary in youth, in age paling into the ritual and thaumaturgic! *When we Dead Awaken*, the awesome whispered confession of the production-man, bemoaning his late, too late declaration of love to life—and *Parsifal*, that oratorio of redemption: how prone I am to think of the two together, to feel them as one, these two farewell mystery plays, last words before the eternal silence! Both of them apocalyptic climaxes, majestic in their sclerotic languor, in the mechanical rigour of their technique, their general tone of reviewing life and casting up accounts, their self-quotation, their flavour of dissolution.

What we used to call *fin-de-siècle*, what was it but the miserable satyr-play of a smaller time, compared with the true and awe-inspiring end of the epoch whose swan-song was the last work of these two great wizards? For Northern wizards were they both, crafty old weavers of spells, profoundly versed in all the arts of insinuation and fascination wielded by a devil's artistry as sensuous as consummate; great in the organisation of effects, in the cult of detail, in all sorts of shifting meanings and symbolic senses, in the exploitation of fancy, the poetising of the intellectual ; and musicians they were to boot, as men of the North should be. Not only the one who consciously acquired his music because he thought it might be useful in his career of conquest ; but also the other, though only privately, through the intellect and as a second string to his mastery of the word.

But what makes them even to bewilderment alike, is the way each subjected to an undreamed-of process of sublimation a form of art which, in both cases, stood at the time at rather a low ebb. In Wagner's case the form was opera, in Ibsen's the social drama. Goethe says : "Everything perfect of its kind must go beyond its kind, it must be something else, incomparable. In some tones the nightingale is still bird ; then it surmounts its species, seeming to want to show to every other feathered fowl what singing really is." In just this sense, Wagner and Ibsen made the opera and the social drama consummate ; they made something else, incomparable, out of them. The other half of the comparison also rings true : sometimes, and sometimes even in *Parsifal*, Wagner is still opera ; sometimes in Ibsen you can hear the creaking of the Dumas technique. But both are creative, in that sense of perfection and consummation ; they have it in common, that they took the accepted and made out of it something new, something undreamed-of.

What is it that raises the works of Wagner to a

plane so high, intellectually speaking, above all other musical drama? Two forces contribute, forces and gifts of genius, which one thinks of in general as opposed, indeed the present day takes pleasure in asserting their essential incompatibility. I mean psychology and the myth. Indeed, psychology does seem too much a matter of reason to admit of our seeing in it anything but an obstacle on the path into the land of myth. And it passes as the antithesis of the mythical as of the musical—yet precisely this complex, of psychology, myth and music, is what confronts us, an organic reality, in two great cases, Nietzsche and Wagner. A book might be written on Wagner the psychologist, on the psychology of his art as musician not less than as poet—in so far as the two are to be separated in him.

The technique of the motif had already been used on occasion in the old opera; it was now gradually built up, by the profoundest virtuosity, into a system which made music more than ever the instrument of psychological allusion, association, emphasis. Wagner's treatment of the love-potion theme, originally the simple epic idea of a magic draught, is the creation of a great psychologist. For actually it might as well be pure water that the lovers drink, and it is only their belief that they have drunk death which frees their souls from the moral compulsion of their day. From the beginning Wagner's poetry goes beyond the bounds of suitability for his libretto—though not so much in the language as precisely in the psychology displayed. "The sombre glow" sings the Dutchman in the fine duet with Senta in the second act:

> "The sombre glow I feel within me burning—
> Shall I, O wretch, confess it for love's yearning ?
> Ah, no, it is salvation that I crave—
> Might such an angel come my soul to save !"

The lines are singable ; but never before had such a complex thought been sung or been written for singing. The devoted man loves this maid at first sight ; but tells himself that his emotion has nothing to do with her. Instead it has to do with his redemption and release. Then confronting her again as the embodiment of his hopes for salvation, he neither can nor will distinguish between the two longings he feels. For his hope has taken on her shape and he can no longer wish it to have another. In plain words, he sees and loves redemption in this maiden—what interweaving of alternatives is here, what a glimpse into the painful abysses of emotion ! This is analysis —and the word comes up in an even bolder and more modern sense when we think of the youthful Siegfried, and the way Wagner vitalises, in his verse and against the significant background of the music, the spring-like germination, the budding and shooting up of that young life and love. It is a pregnant complex, gleaming up from the unconscious, of mother-fixation, sexual desire and fear—the fairy-story fear, I mean, that Siegfried wanted so to feel: a complex which displays Wagner the psychologist in remarkable intuitive agreement with another typical son of the nineteenth century, the psycho-analyst Sigmund Freud. When Siegfried dreams under the linden tree and the mother-idea flows into the erotic; when Mime teaches his pupil the nature of fear, while the orchestra down below darkly and afar off introduces the fire-motif: all that is Freud, that is analysis, nothing else—and we recall that Freud, whose profound investigation into the roots and depths of mind has been, in its broadest lines, anticipated by Nietzsche, shows an interest in the mythical, precultural and primeval which is narrowly associated with the psychological.

"Love in fullest reality," says Wagner, "is only possible within sex; only as man and woman can human beings love most genuinely, all other love is derivative, having reference to this or artificially modelled upon it. It is false to think of this love (the sexual) as only one manifestation of love in general, other and perhaps higher manifestations being presumed beside it." This reduction of all love to the sexual has an unmistakably psycho-analytical character. It shows the same psychological naturalism as Schopenhauer's metaphysical formula of the "focus of the will" and Freud's cultural theories and his theory of sublimation. It is genuine nineteenth century.

The erotic mother-complex appears again in *Parsifal*, in the seduction-scene in the second act—and here we come to Kundry, the boldest, most powerful creation among Wagner's figures—he himself probably felt how extraordinary she was. Not Kundry but the emotions proper to Good Friday were Wagner's original point of departure; but gradually his ideas more and more took shape about her, and the decisive conception of the dual personality, the thought of making the wild *Gralsbotin* (messenger of the Grail) one and the same being with the beguiling temptress, supplied the final inspiration—and betrays the secret depths of the fascination that drew him to so strange an enterprise.

"Since this occurred to me," he writes, "almost everything about the material has become clear." And again: "In particular I see more and more vividly and compellingly a strange creation, a wonderful world-demonic female (the *Gralsbotin*). If I manage to finish this piece of work it will be something highly original." Original—that is a touchingly subdued and modest word for the result he actually produced. Wagner's heroines are in general marked by a trait of lofty hysteria; they have something sleep-walking, ecstatic and prophetic which imparts an odd, uncanny modernity to their romantic heroics. But Kundry herself, the Rose of Hell, is definitely a piece of mythical pathology; her tortured and distracted duality, now as *instrumentum diaboli*, now as salvation-seeking penitent, is portrayed with clinical ruthlessness and realism, with a naturalistic boldness of perception and depiction in the morbid realm, that has always seemed to me the uttermost limit of knowledge and mastery. And Kundry is not the only character in *Parsifal* with this excessive type of mentality. The draft of this last work of Wagner says of Klingsor that he is the demon of the hidden sin, he is impotence raging against evil—and here we are transported into a Christian world that takes cognisance of recondite and infernal soul-states, in short, into the world of Dostoiewsky.

Our second phenomenon is Wagner as mythologist, as discoverer of the myth for purposes of the opera, as saviour of the opera through the myth. And truly he has not his like for soul-affinity with this picture-world of thought, nor his equal in the power of invoking and reanimating the myth. When he forsook the historical opera for the myth he found himself; and listening to him one is fain to believe that music was made for nothing else, nor could have any other mission but to serve mythology. Whether as messenger from a purer sphere, sent to the aid of innocence and then, alas, since faith proves inconstant, withdrawing thither whence it came; or as lore, spoken and sung, of the world's beginning and end, a sort of cosmogonic fairy-tale philosophy—in all this the spirit of the myth, its essence and its key, are struck with a certainty, an elective intuition; its very language is spoken with a native-bornness that has not its like in all art. It is the language of "once upon a time" in the double sense of "as it always was" and "as it always shall be"; the density of the mythological atmosphere—as in the scene with the Norns, at the beginning of the *Götterdämmerung*, where the three daughters of Erda indulge in a solemn-faced gossip about the state of the world, or in the appearances of Erda herself in the *Rheingold* and *Siegfried*—is unsurpassable. The overpowering accents of the music that bears away Siegfried's corpse no longer refer to the woodland youth who set forth in order to learn fear ; they instruct our feeling in what is really passing there behind falling veils of mist. The sun-hero himself lies on his bier, struck down by blind darkness, and the word comes to the aid of our emotions : "the fury of a wild boar," it says, and "he is the accursed boar," says Gunther, pointing to Hagen, "who mangled the flesh of this noble youth." A perspective opens out into the first and furthest of our human picture-dreamings. Tammuz, Adonis whom the boar slew, Osiris, Dionysius, the dismembered ones, who are to return as the Crucified whose side a Roman spear must pierce that men may know him—all that was and ever is, the whole world of slain and martyred loveliness this mythic gaze encompasses ; and so let no one say that he who created Siegfried was through Parsifal untrue to himself.

My passion for the Wagnerian enchantment began with me so soon as I knew of it, and began to make it my own and to penetrate it with my understanding. All that I owe to him, of enjoyment and instruction, I can never forget : the hours of deep and single bliss in the midst of the theatre crowds, hours of nervous and intellectual transport and rapture, of insights of great and moving import such as only this art vouchsafes. My zeal is never weary, I am never satiated, with watching, listening, admiring—not, I confess, without misgivings; but the doubts and objections do my zeal as little wrong as did Nietzsche's immortal critique, which has always seemed to me like a panegyric with the wrong label, like another kind of glorification. It was love-in-hate, it was self-flagellation. Wagner's art was the great passion of Nietzsche's life. He loved it as did Baudelaire, the poet of the *Fleurs du Mal*, of whom it is told that in the agony, the paralysis and the clouded mind of his last days, he smiled with pleasure when he heard Wagner's name: "*il a souri d'allégresse.*" Thus Nietzsche in his paralytic night, used to listen to the sound of that name, and say: "I loved him very much." He hated him very much too, on intellectual, cultural, ethical grounds—which shall not be mentioned, here and now, on that "sacred day," as Nietzsche called it, on which Wagner died in Venice. But it would be strange indeed if I stood alone in the feeling that Nietzsche's polemic against Wagner whips up enthusiasm for the composer rather than paralyses it.

What I did take exception to, always—or rather, what left me cold—was Wagner's theory. It is hard for me to believe that anyone ever took it seriously. This combination of music, speech, painting, gesture, that gave itself out to be the only true art and the fulfilment of all artistic yearning—what had I to do with this? A theory of art which would make *Tasso* give way to *Siegfried*? I found it hard to swallow, this derivation of the single arts from the disintegration of an original theatrical unity, to which they should all happily find their way back. Art is entire and complete in each of its forms and manifestations; we do not need to add up the different species to make a whole. To think that, is *bad* nineteenth century, a bad, mechanistic mode of thought; and Wagner's triumphant performance does not justify his theory but only itself. It lives, and it will live, but art will outlive it in the arts, and move mankind through them, as it always has. We should be children and barbarians to suppose that the influence of art upon us is profounder or loftier by reason of the heaped-up volume of its assault upon our senses.

Wagner, as an impassioned man of the theatre—one might call him a theatromaniac—inclined to such a belief, in so far as the first desideratum of art appeared to him to be the most immediate and complete communication to the senses of everything that was to be said. And strange enough it is to see, in the case of his principal work, *The Ring of the Nibelungs*, what was the effect of this ruthless demand of his upon the drama, which after all was the crux of all his striving, and of which the fundamental law seemed to him to be precisely this utter, all-inclusive sense-appeal. We know the story of how this work was written. Wagner was working on his dramatic sketch of Siegfried's death; he himself tells us that he found it intolerable to have so much of the story lying before the beginning of the play, which had then to be woven in afterwards as it proceeded. He felt an overpowering need to bring that previous history within the sphere of his sense-appeal, and so he began to write backwards: first *Young Siegfried*, then the *Valkyrie*, then the *Rheingold*. He rested not until he had reduced the past to the present and brought it all upon the stage—in four evenings, everything from the primitive cell, the primeval beginnings, the first E-major of the bass bassoon at the commencement of the overture to the *Rheingold*, with which then he solemnly and almost soundlessly set to. Something glorious was the result, and we can understand the enthusiasm of its creator in view of the success of a scheme so colossal, so rich in new and profound possibilities of effectiveness. But what was it, really, this result? Æsthetics has been known to repudiate the composite drama as an art-form. Grillparzer, for instance, did so. He considered that the relation of one part to another resulted in imparting an epic character to the whole—whereby, indeed, it gained in sublimity. But precisely this is what conditions the effectiveness of the *Ring* and the nature of its greatness: Wagner's masterpiece owes its sublimity to the epic spirit, and the epic is the sphere from which its material is drawn. The *Ring* is a scenic epic ; its source is the dislike of the previous histories that haunt the stage behind the scenes—a dislike not shared, as we know, by the classic nor by the French drama. Ibsen is much closer to the classic stage, with his analytical technique and his skill at developing the previous histories. It is amusing to think that precisely Wagner's theory of dramatic sense-appeal was what so wonderfully betrayed him into the epic vein.

His relation to the single arts out of which he created his "composite art-work" is worth dwelling upon. It has something peculiarly dilettantish about it. In the still loyal fourth *Thoughts Out of Season* (*Unzeitgemässe Betrachtungen*) upon Wagner's childhood and youth, Nietzsche says : "His youth is that of a many-sided dilettante, of whom nothing very much will come. He had no strict, inherited family tradition to make a frame for him. Painting, poetry, acting, music, came as naturally to him as an academic career ; the superficial observer might think him a born dilettante." In fact, not only the superficial but the admiring and empassioned observer might well say, at risk of being misunderstood, that Wagner's art *is* dilettantism, monumentalised and lifted into the sphere of genius by his intelligence and his enormous will-power. There is something dilettante in the very idea of a union of the arts ; it could never have got beyond the dilettante had they not one and all been ruthlessly subordinated to his vast genius for expression. There is something suspect in his relation to the arts—something unæsthetic, however nonsensical that may sound. Italy, the plastic and graphic arts, leave him cold. He writes to Frau Wesendonck in Rome: "See everything for me too—I need to have somebody do it for me. . . . I have my own way of responding to these things, as I have discovered again and again, and finally quite conclusively when I was in Italy. For a while I am vividly impressed by some significant visual experience; but—it does not last. It seems that my eyes are not enough for me to use to take in the world."

Perfectly understandable. For he is an ear-man, a musician and poet; but still it is odd that he can write from Paris to the same correspondent: "Well, well, how the child is revelling in Raphael and painting! All very lovely, sweet and soothing; only it never touches me. I am still the Vandal who, in a whole year spent in Paris, never got round to visit the Louvre. That tells the whole story." Not the whole; but after all something, and that something is significant. Painting is a great art—as great as the composite art work. It existed before the composite art work and it continues to do so—but it moves him not. He would have to be smaller than he is, for one not to be wounded to the heart for the art of painting! For neither as past nor as living present has it anything to say to him. The great French impressionistic school grew up beside him, as it were—he hardly saw it; it had nothing to do with him. His relations with it were confined to the fact that Renoir painted his portrait; not a very flattering portrait—we are told that he did not much care for it. But his attitude toward poetry was clearly different. Throughout his life it gave him infinite riches—especially Shakespeare; though he speaks contemptuously of "literature-writers" in defence of the theory by which he glorifies his own powers. But no matter for that; he has made mighty contribution to poetry, she is much the richer for his work—always bearing in mind that it must not be read, that it is not really written verse but, as it were, exhalations from the music, needing to be complemented by gesture, music and picture and existing as poetry only when all these work together. Purely as composition it is often bombastic, baroque, even childish; it has something majestically and sovereignly inept—side by side with such passages of absolute genius, power, compression, primeval beauty, as disarm all doubt; though they never quite make us forget that what we have here are images that stand not within the cultural structure of our great European literature and poetry, but apart from it, more in the nature of directions for a theatrical performance which among other things needs a text. Among such gems of language interspersed among the boldly dilettante, I think in particular of the *Ring* and of *Lohengrin*—the latter, purely as writing, is perhaps the noblest, purest and finest of Wagner's achievements.

His genius lies in a dramatic synthesis of the arts, which only as a whole, precisely as a synthesis, answers to our conception of a genuine and legitimate work of art. The component parts—even to the music, in itself, not considered as part of a whole—breathe something irregular, over-grown, that only disappears when they blend into the noble whole. Wagner's relation to his language is not that of our great poets and writers, it wants the severity and delicacy displayed by those who find in words the highest good and the most trusted medium of art. That is proved by his occasional poems ; the sugared and romantic adulations of Ludwig II of Bavaria, the banal and jolly jingles addressed to helpers and friends. One single careless little rhyme of Goethe is pure gold—and pure literature—compared with these versified platitudes and hearty masculine jests, at which our reverence for Wagner can only make us smile rather ruefully. Let us keep to Wagner's prose, to the manifestos and self-expositions on æsthetic and cultural matters. They are essays of astonishing mental virility, but they are not to be compared, as literary and intellectual achievements, with Schiller's works on the philosophy of art—for instance, that immortal essay on *Naive and Sentimental Poetry*. They are hard to read, their style is both stiff and confused, again there is something about them that is overgrown, extraneous, dilettante : they do not belong to the sphere of great German and European prose ; they are not the work of a born writer, but the casual product of some necessity. With Wagner everything was like that, always the product of necessity. Happy, devoted, complete, legitimate and great he is, only in the mass.

Then was his musicianship too only the product of the demands made upon him by the whole overpowering product, only the result of strength of will ? Nietzsche says somewhere that the so-called "gift" cannot be the essential thing about genius. "For instance," he cries, "what very little gift Richard Wagner had ! Was ever a musician so poor as he still was in his twenty-eighth year ?" And it is true that Wagner's musical beginnings were all timid, uncertain and partial, and lie much later in his life than is usually the case. He himself says : "I still remember, round my thirtieth year, asking myself whether I possessed the instrument to develop an artistic individuality of high rank ; I could still trace in my work a tendency to imitation, and looked forward only with great anxiety to my development as an independent original creator." That is a retrospect, he wrote it as a master, in 1862. But only three years earlier, in Lucerne, he had days when he simply could not get forward with the *Tristan* ; he writes to Liszt : "How pathetic I seem to myself as a musician I cannot find words strong enough to tell you. At the bottom of my heart, I feel an absolute tyro. You should see me sitting here, thinking 'It simply *must* go' ; then I go to the piano and dig out some wretched trash, only to throw it away again. Imagine my feelings, my inward conviction of my utter musical incapacity. And now you come, oozing it out of all your pores, streams and springs and waterfalls of it, and I have to listen to what you say of me! Not to believe that it is sheer irony, is very hard. Dear man, this is a singular story, and believe me, I am no great shakes." That is pure depression, irrelevant in every word, and doubly absurd in the address to which it went. Liszt answers it as it should be answered. He reproaches him with "frantic injustice toward himself." Every artist knows this sudden shame, felt on confronting some masterly performance. For the practice of an art always, in every case, means a fresh and very careful adaptation of the personal and individual to the art in general; thus a man, even after he has received recognition for happy performances of his own, can suddenly compare them with the work of others and ask himself, "Is it possible to mention my own adaptation in the same breath with these things?" Even so, such a degree of depressive self-depreciation, such pangs of conscience in the face of music, in a man who is in the middle of the third act of *Tristan*—there is something strange about it, something psychologically remarkable. Truly he had paid with a deal of poor-spirited self-abasement for the dictatorial self-sufficiency of his later days, when he published in the Bayreuth papers so much scorn and condemnation of the beautiful in Mendelssohn, Schumann, Brahms, to the greater glory of his own art! What was the source of these attacks of faint-heartedness? They could only come from the error he made at such moments: of isolating his musicianship and thus bringing it into comparison with the best, whereas it should only be regarded *sub specie* of his whole creative production—and vice-versa; to this error is due all the embittered opposition which his music had to overcome. We, who owe to this wonder-world of sound, to this intellectual wizardry, so much bliss and ravishment, so much amazement at sight of this giant capacity, self-created—we find it hard to understand the opposition and the repulsion. The expressions that were used, descriptions like "cold," "algebraic," "formless," seem to us shockingly uncomprehending and lacking in insight; with a want of receptivity, a thick-skinned poverty of understanding that inclines us to think they could only have come from Philistine spheres, forsaken alike of God and music. But no. Many of those who so judged, who were impelled so to judge, were no Philistines, they were artistic spirits, musicians and lovers of music, who had her interest at heart and could with justice claim that they were able to distinguish between the musical and the unmusical. And they found that this music was no music. Their opinion has been completely counted out, it has suffered a mass defeat. But even if it was false, was it also inexcusable? Wagner's music is not music, to the same extent that the dramatic basis (which unites with it to form a creative art) is not literature. It is psychology, symbolism, mythology, emphasis, everything—only not music in the pure and consummate sense intended by those bewildered critics. The texts round which it twines, filling out their dramatic content, are not literature —but the music is! Like a geyser it seems to shoot forth out of the myth's precultural depths—and not only seems, for it actually does it—and in very truth it is conceived, deliberately, calculatedly, with high intelligence, with an extreme of shrewdness, in a spirit as literary as the spirit of the texts is musical. Music, resolved into its primeval elements, must serve to force philosophic conclusions into high relief. The ever-craving chromatics of the *Liebestod* are a literary idea. The Rhine's immemorial flow, the seven primitive chords—like blocks to build up Walhalla—are no less so. I walked home one night with a famous conductor who had just finished conducting *Tristan*; he said to me, "That is not even music any more." He voiced the sense of our common emotion. But what we said with acceptance, with admiration, could not but have sounded in the beginning like a furious denial. Such music as Siegfried's Rhine journey, or the Funeral March, of unspeakable glory for our ears, for our spirits, they were never listened to, they were unheard-of in the worst sense of the phrase. This stringing together of symbolic musical quotations, till they lie like boulders in the stream of musical development—it was too much to ask that they be considered music as Bach, Beethoven and Mozart are music. Too much to ask that the E-major triad at the beginning of the *Rheingold* be called music. It was not. It was an acoustic idea : the idea of the beginning of all things. It was the self-willed dilettante's exploitation of music to express a mythological idea. Psychoanalysis claims to know that love is composed and put together out of elements of sheer perversity ; yet, and therefore, she remains love, the most divine this world has to show. Well, now, the genius of Richard Wagner is put together out of streams of dilettantism.

But what streams ! He is a musician who can persuade even the unmusical to be musical. That may be a drawback in the eyes of *illuminati* and aristocrats of the art. But when among the unmusical we find men like Baudelaire— ? For him, contact with the world of music was simply contact with Wagner. He wrote to Wagner that he had no understanding of music, and knew none except a few fine things by Weber and Beethoven. And now, he felt an ecstasy which made him want to make music with words alone, to vie with Wagner in language—all of which had far-reaching consequences for French poetry. A pseudo-music, a dilettante musician, can do with converts and proselytes such as this ; even the austerest music might envy them—and not them alone. For there are things in this popular music, so splendid, so full of genius, as to make such distinctions ridiculous. The swan motif in *Lohengrin* and *Parsifal*, the summer full moon music at the end of the second act of the *Meistersinger* and the quintet in the third act ; the A-major harmony in the second act of *Tristan*, and Tristan's visions of the lovers crossing the sea ; the Good Friday music in *Parsifal* and the mighty transformation music in the third act ; the glorious duet between Siegfried and Brunnhilde at the beginning of the *Götterdämmerung*, with the folk-song cadence ; "*Willst Du mir Minne schenken*" and the ravishing "*Heil Dir Brunnhilde, prangender Stern*" ; certain parts from the Venusberg revision of the *Tristan* time—these are inspirations which might make absolute music flush with delight or grow pale with envy. I have selected them at random. There are many others which I might have cited, to display Wagner's astonishing skill in modifying, modulating and re-interpreting a motif already introduced : for instance, in the prelude to the third act of the *Meistersinger*, where Hans Sachs' *Schusterlied*, already known to us from the humorous second act as a lusty workman's song, is lifted to unexpected heights of poetry. Or take the recasting —of rhythm and timbre—and the restatement which the so-called faith-motif undergoes ; we hear it first in the overture and many times throughout the *Parsifal*, beginning with Gurnemanz's great recitative. It is hard to refer to these things with only words at one's disposition. Why, as I think of Wagner's music, does some small detail, a mere flourish, wake in my ear, like the horn-figure, technically quite easy to describe, and yet quite indescribable, which in the lament for Siegfried's death harmonically foreshadows the love-motif of his parents? At such moments one scarcely knows whether it is Wagner's own peculiar and personal art, or music itself, that one so loves, that so charms one. In a word, it is heavenly—though only music could make one take the gushing adjective in one's mouth without shame.

The general tone, psychologically speaking, of Wagner's music is heavy, pessimistic, laden with sluggish yearning, broken in rhythm; it seems to be wrestling up out of darkness and confusion to redemption in the beautiful; it is the music of a burdened soul, it has no dancing appeal to the muscles, it struggles, urges and drives most labouredly, most unsouthernly—Lenbach's quick wit characterised it aptly when he said to Wagner one day: "Your music—dear me, it is a sort of luggage van to the kingdom of heaven." But it is not only that. Its soul-heaviness must not make one forget that it can also produce the sprightly, blithe and stately—as in the themes of the knights, the motifs of Lohengrin, Stolzing and Parsifal, the natural mischievousness and fated loveliness of the terzetto of the Rhine maidens, the burlesque humour and learned arrogance of the overture to the *Meistersinger*, the jolly folk-music of the dance in the second act. Wagner can do anything. In the art of characterisation he is incomparable; to understand his music as a method of characterisation is to admire it without stint. It is picturesque, it is even grotesque ; it is all based upon the perspective required by the theatre. But it has a richness of inventiveness even in small matters, a flexible capacity of entering into character, speech and gesture, such as was never seen in so marked a degree. In the single rôles it is triumphant : take the figure of the Flying Dutchman, musically and poetically encompassed by doom and destruction, wrapped round by the wild raging of the lonely seas. Or Loki with his elemental incalculableness and malicious charm, or Siegfried's dwarf foster-father, knock-kneed and blinking ; or Beckmesser's silly spite. It is the Dionysiac play-actor and his art—his arts, if you like—revealing themselves in this omnipotent, ubiquitous power of depiction and transformation. He changes not only his human mask, he enters into nature and speaks in the tempest and the thunder-bolt, in the rustling leaf and the sparkling wave, in the rainbow and the dancing flame. Alberic's tarn-cap is the comprehensive symbol of this genius for disguise, this imitative all-pervasiveness : that can enter as well into the spongy hopping and crawling of the lowly toad as into the care-free, cloud-swinging existence of the old Norse gods. It is this characteristic versatility that could encompass works of such absolute heterogeneity as the *Meistersinger*, sturdy and German as Luther himself, and *Tristan's* death-drunken, death-yearning world. It marks off each of the operas from the others, develops each out of one fundamental note which distinguishes it from all the rest; so that—within the entire product, which after all is a personal cosmos—each single work forms a closed and starry cosmos of its own. Among them are musical contacts and relations that indicate the organic nature of the whole. Accents of the *Meistersinger* are heard in *Parsifal*; in the *Flying Dutchman* we get anticipations of *Lohengrin*, and in its text hints of the religious raptures of *Parsifal*, as in the words, "*Ein heil'ger Balsam meinen Wunden*," "*Der Schwur, dem hohen Wort entfliesst*." And in the Christian *Lohengrin* there is a pagan residuum, personified by Ortrud, that suggests the *Ring*. But on the whole each work is stylistically set off against the rest, in a way that makes one see and almost feel the secret of style as the very kernel of art, well-nigh as art itself: the secret of the union of the personal with the objective. In every one of his works Wagner is quite himself, not a beat therein could be by anybody else, each bears his unmistakable formula and signature. And yet each is at the same time stylistically a world of its own, the product of an objective intuition which holds the balance with the personal will-power and is entirely resolved in it. Perhaps the greatest marvel in this respect is the work of the seventy-year-old man, the *Parsifal*: here the uttermost is achieved in exploring and expressing remote and awful and holy worlds—yes, *Tristan* notwithstanding this is the uttermost point reached by Wagner, it witnesses to a power of blending style and emotion even beyond his usual capacity ; to these sounds one surrenders with ever new interest, unrest and bewitchment.

"A bad business, this," writes Wagner from Lucerne in 1859, in the midst of his absorbing labours on the third act of *Tristan*, which have renewed his interest in the long-since envisaged and already sketched figure of Amfortas. "A bad business ! Think of it, for God's sake : it has suddenly become frightfully plain to me that Amfortas is my Tristan of the third act, at his unthinkable culmination." This process of "culmination" is the involuntary law of the life and growth of Wagner's productions, and it is the result of self-indulgence. All his life long he was labouring to utter Amfortas, in accents broken by torment and sin. He was already there in Tannhäuser's "Ah, how the weight of sin oppresses me !" In *Tristan* they seem to have reached their uttermost and shattering expression ; but in *Parsifal*, as he recognises himself, with horror, they must undergo another "unthinkable culmination." It is a matter of screwing up his language to the highest pitch and then unconsciously seeking ever stronger and intenser situations to go with them. The material, the single works, are stages and successive transformations of a unity possessed by the self-contained and consummate life-work—which "develops" but to a certain extent was present from the beginning. This is the explanation of the telescoping, the dovetailing of conceptions ; from which it results, in an artist of this kind and calibre, that what he is working on is never merely the task in hand; for everything else is weighing upon him and burdening the productive moment. Something apparently (and only half apparently) planned, planned for a lifetime, comes out when we know that Wagner, in 1862, wrote quite definitely to von Bülow from Bieberich that *Parsifal* would be his last work. This was a round twenty years before it was actually performed. The *Siegfried* will have been sandwiched in between *Tristan* and the *Meistersinger*, and the whole *Ring* worked up, in order to fill in the holes in the scheme. During the whole of *Tristan* he had to carry on at the *Ring*, and in *Tristan*, from the beginning, there are hints of *Parsifal*. The latter was present even during the sound and healthy, Luther-spirited *Meistersinger*; it had been waiting since 1845, the year of the first performance of *Tannhäuser*, in Dresden. In 1848 comes the prose draft which condenses the Nibelung myth into a drama: the putting on paper of *Siegfried's Death*, which was to end in the *Götterdämmerung*. But meantime, between 1846–47, the *Lohengrin* is composed, and the action of the *Meistersinger* drafted, as a satyr-play and humorous pendant to *Tannhäuser*. This fourth decade of the century, in the middle of which he will be thirty-two years old, rounds out the working plan of the whole of his life, which will be carried out in the following four decades up to 1881, all the plays being dovetailed in together by simultaneous working on them all. His work, strictly speaking, has no chronology. It originates, of course, in time; but it is there all at once, and has been there from the beginning. The last achievement, foreseen as such from the beginning, and completed with his sixty-ninth year, is then in so far release, that it means the fulfilment, the end and the exitus, and nothing more comes after it; the old man's work on it, the work of an artist who has entirely lived out his powers, is nothing more than just work on it. The giant task is finished, is complete; the heart, which has held out the storms of seventy years, may, in a last spasm, cease to beat.

This creative burden, then, rested on shoulders which were far from being as broad as Saint Christopher's; on a constitution so weakly, to judge by appearances and by subjective evidence, that no one would have expected it to hold out to carry such a burden to its goal. This nature felt itself every minute on the verge of exhaustion, only by exception did it experience the sensations of well-being. Constipated, melancholy, sleepless, generally tormented, this man is at thirty in such a state that he will often sit down to weep for a quarter of an hour on end. He cannot believe that he will live to see the *Tannhäuser* finished. To undertake at thirty-six to bring the *Ring* to completion seems to him presumption; when he is forty, he "thinks daily of death"—he who will be writing *Parsifal* at almost sixty-nine.

His martyrdom is a nervous complaint, one of

those organically intangible illnesses which make a fool of a man years on end and without being actually dangerous cause life to be a burden to him. It is hard for the victim to believe that they are not dangerous: more than one place in Wagner's letters shows that he regards himself as death-devoted. "My nerves," he writes at thirty-nine to his sister, "are by now in complete decline; it is possible that some change in my outward life will stave off death for some years yet; but cannot stop the process." And in the same year: "I am nervously very ill, and after several efforts at a radical treatment of the disease have come to the conclusion that there is no hope of recovery. My work is all that keeps me up; but the nerves of my brain are already so ruined that I cannot work more than two hours in the day and then only if I lie down for two hours afterwards and perhaps can fall asleep a little." Two hours daily. By such small stages, then, at least at times, this whole gigantic life work is erected; struggling all the time against rapidly supervening exhaustion, complement to a tough elasticity which can in no long time restore the easily exhausted energies. And the moral name of this process is patience. "True patience displays great elasticity," Novalis notes; and Schopenhauer praises it as the genuine courage. It is this moral and physical combination of courage, patience and elasticity that enables this man to carry out his mission; Wagner's history, as scarcely that of any other artist, gives us an insight into the peculiar vital structure of genius : this mixture of sensibility and strength, delicacy and endurance, which is compact of labour against odds and all-unexpected rewards, and out of which great works come. It is not surprising that in time it displays a sense of being kept on through the self-will of the task itself. It is hard not to believe in a metaphysical wifulness of the work which is struggling towards realisation, whose tool and willing-unwilling victim the author is. "Truly I do very wretchedly indeed, but I do"—that is a despairing, self-mocking cry out of one of Wagner's letters. And he does not fail to set up a causal nexus between his sufferings and his art ; he recognises art and illness to be one and the same affliction—with the result that he tries to escape from them, naïvely, by the help of a water-cure. "A year ago," he writes, "I found myself in a hydropathic establishment, where I hoped and wanted to become an entirely healthy man by the healing of my senses. I was wishing for the kind of health that would make it possible for me to get rid of art, the martyrdom of my life ; it was a last desperate struggle for happiness, for real, respectable joy in life, such as only healthy people can have."

How touching is this confused and childish utterance ! He looks to have cold water cure him of art, that is, from the constitution which makes him an artist. His relation to art, which is his destiny, is complex almost beyond hope of unravelling, highly contradictory, involved—sometimes he fairly seems to be quivering in the meshes of a logical net. "So I am to do this too?" cries the forty-six-year-old man, after going at length and with animation into the symbolic and intellectual content of the *Parisfal* plan. "And music for it too! Thanks very much. Whoever wants to may do it, I'll fight it off as long as I can." The words have an accent of feminine coquetry; they are full of trembling eagerness for the work, awareness of the inward voice "Thou must," and the voluptuous pleasure of denial. The dream of getting free, of living instead of creating, of being happy, continues to recur in the letters; the words happiness, disinterested happiness, noble enjoyment of life are everywhere expressed as the opposite to the artist existence; as also the conception of art as substitute for all direct forms of enjoyment. At thirty-nine he writes to Liszt: "I decline more and more surely from day to day. I lead *an indescribably worthless life.* Of real enjoyment of life I know nothing; for me enjoyment, *love* [he underlines the word] are imaginary, not experienced. My heart had to be absorbed in my brain, my life had to become artificial; now I can only live as 'artist,' all the human being is absorbed in that." We must admit that never before has art been characterised in stronger words, in more desperate frankness, as drug, intoxicant, *paradis artificiel.* And he has attacks of violent revolt against this artificial existence, as on his fortieth birthday, when he writes to Liszt: "I want to be baptized anew; will you be godfather? I'd like for us both to get clean away, out into the world! Come out with me into the wide world—even if we just went gaily to smash there, and sank into some abyss!" One thinks of Tannhäuser, clinging to Wolfram to drag him away to the Venusberg; for certainly the world and "life" are, as in a fever-dream of renunciation, conceived as the Venusberg, as a state of thorough-going Bohemian *je m'en fichisme* and the self-destruction of mad dissipation—in short, as all that for which art offers him a "worthless" substitute.

On the other hand, or rather in strange alternation with this, art appears to him in a quite different light: as a means of release, as sedative, as a condition of pure contemplation and surrender of the will; for thus philosophy taught him to regard it, and with the docility and goodwill common to children and artists he was anxious to obey. Oh, he is idealist! Life has its meaning not in itself but in the higher things, the task, the creative activity, and thus "to be forever struggling to produce what is needed" as he is, "to be often for long periods of time unable to think of aught but how I must act in order to get outward peace for even a little while and get hold of what is necessary for existence, and to that end to have to depart so utterly out of my own character, to have to appear to people from whom I need things to be so entirely different from what I am—that is really maddening. . . . All these cares are so fit and natural to the man to whom life is an end in itself, who gets all the joy he finds in things out of the trouble he has to take to bring them about, and who can simply never understand why that is so absolutely disgusting to the likes of us, since it is the common lot of mankind! That anybody should look on life as not an end in itself, but as an indispensable means to a higher goal—who really does understand that at the bottom of his soul?" (Letter to Mathilde Wesendonck, Venice, 1858.) In truth, it is a shameful and degrading thing to be obliged to fight for life like that, to go on one's knees for it, when life itself is not at all what one wants, but one's higher goal lying above and outside life: art, creation, for whose sake one must fight for rest and peace, and which themselves appear in the light of rest and peace. And even when one has finally by dint of struggling achieved the conditions for work—which are not so easily satisfied—then only begins the actual and higher voluntary drudgery, the productive struggle involved in art. For what he fancied, in his deluded philosophising while he struggled for the baser ends of existence, to be pure "idea" and redeeming wisdom, proves to be the real wheel of Ixion, the last and uttermost convulsion of the labouring will.

Purity and peace—a deep craving for these two lies in his breast, complementary to his thirst for life. And when the craving reacts against his attempt to seize upon immediate pleasure, then art —it is a fresh complication in his relations to her—

appears to him in the light of a hindrance to his healing. What we have here is a variation of the Tolstoian repudiation of art, the cruel denial of one's own natural endowment, for the sake of the "spirit." Ah, art! How right was Buddha, when he called it the broadest path that leads away from salvation! There is a long and tempestuous letter written from Venice to Frau Wesendonck, in 1858, in which he sets this forth to his friend, in discussing his idea of a Buddhistic drama. "Buddhistic drama"—there was precisely the difficulty. It is a contradiction in terms—as had become clear to him when he tried to utilise dramatically, and in particular musically, the idea of a being utterly free, lifted above all passions, such as the Buddha was. The pure and holy one, through knowledge tranquillised, is, artistically speaking dead—that was quite clear. It was a piece of good luck that, according to the sources, Sha-kya Muni Buddha had a last problem to face, was involved in a final conflict: he had to come to the conclusion, despite his former principles, to receive the Dragon's Daughter into the company of the elect. And thus, thank God, he became a possible subject for artistic treatment. Wagner rejoices; but at the same moment the life-bound nature of all art, the knowledge of her temptress power, falls heavily upon his conscience. Has he not already caught her in the act of preferring the play and not the spirit? Without art he might be a saint, with her he never will. If the highest knowledge and the deepest insight were vouchsafed him, it could only make him what he was, a poet, an artist; they would stand there before him, soulfully evident, an enchanting picture, and he would not be able to resist giving it created being. Worse yet, he would even take pleasure in the devilish antinomy! It is horrible—but fascinatingly interesting—one might make a romantic psychological opera out of it—and that, more or less, is what Wagner has done, in the letter to Frau Wesendonck, which is a sort of first draft. Goethe asserts: "One cannot withdraw from the world more securely than through art, one cannot knit oneself more securely to it than through her." That tranquil and comforting statement—see what becomes of it in the head of a romantic!

But whatever guise art adopts, and whether she is a betrayal of the joys alike of sense and of salvation, in any case the work goes on, thanks to that elastic power of recovery which he himself must admire in secret; the scores pile up, and that is the main thing. This man knows as little as do any of us the right way of living. He *is lived*, life squeezes from him what it wants, that is to say, his works, regardless of the mazes his thought wanders in. "My child, this *Tristan* is getting *frightful*! This last act! I am afraid the opera will be forbidden—if the whole thing is not to become a burlesque through bad production. Only mediocre production can save me. Too good would make people crazy. I cannot imagine it otherwise. I have been driven as far as this! Alas! I was just in full train—adieu!" A note to Frau Wesendonck. A quite un-Buddhistic note, full of excited, half-terrified laughter at the madness and badness of what he is doing. This infirm and melancholic man—what a fund of good temper, what indestructible resiliency he must have possessed! His disease, after all, consists in being a variation of the bourgeois variety of health. He gave out a vital magic that made Nietzsche call association with him the one great joyful experience of his life. And he had, before everything else, the inestimable power of throwing emotion on one side and giving free rein to the commonplace. Among his artists in Bayreuth, after a day of strenuous labour, he would announce the advent of rest and relaxation, crying out, "Now not another serious word!" He understood them perfectly, these little theatrical people whom he needed for the realisation of his ideas; despite the great intellectual disparity, he was himself theatre-blood through and through, a comrade of the Thespian car. His simple-minded friend Heckel from Mannheim, the first shareholder of Bayreuth, tells priceless things on this subject. "Very often," he writes, "the relations between Wagner and his artists were extremely jolly and free-and-easy. At the last rehearsal in the salon of the Hôtel Sommer he actually, out of sheer high spirits, stood on his head." Again one thinks of Tolstoi: I mean the time when the grey-bearded prophet and melancholic Christian felt such a superabundance of vitality that he actually jumped up on his father-in-law's shoulder. One is no less artist than are the tenors and soubrettes that call one master: a human creature inclined—at bottom—to being and making merry, an instigator to all kinds of festivities and diversions—in profound and most healthful contrast to the wise and knowledgeable and commanding intelligence, the perfectly serious human being, like Nietzsche. It is well to understand that the artist, even he inhabiting the most austere regions of art, is *not* an absolutely serious man; that effects and enjoyment are his stock-in-trade, and that tragedy and farce can spring from one and the same root. A turn of the lighting changes one into the other; the farce is a hidden tragedy, the tragedy—in the last analysis—a sublime practical joke. The seriousness of the artist—a subject to ponder. And perhaps to shudder at—if what we mean is the intellectual veracity of the artist being, for his artistic veracity, the famous "serious playing"—that purest, loftiest and most moving manifestation of the human mind—does not come in here. But the other, what is to be said for it: and in particular for the seriousness of that seeker after truth, that thinker and believer Richard Wagner? The ascetic and Christian ideals of his later period, the sacramental philosophy of salvation won by abstinence from fleshly lusts of every kind; the convictions and opinions of which *Parsifal* is the expression; even *Parsifal* itself—all these incontestably deny, revoke, cancel the sensualism and the revolutionary spirit of Wagner's young days, which pervade the whole atmosphere and content of the *Siegfried.* It did not, it might not exist any longer. If the artist was intellectually sincere in these new, later and probably definitive views, then the works of the earlier epochs, recognised as erroneous, sinful and pernicious, must have been denounced and extirpated, burned by their creator's very hand, so as not to be any longer a stumbling-block to humanity. But he does not think of it—actually the idea does not even occur to him. Who could destroy such beautiful compositions ? So they continue to exist, side by side, and they continue to be played ; for the artist has reverence for his biography. He yields himself to the varying psychological moods of life as it passes, and portrays them in works which to the eye of reason may contradict each other, but are individually all beautiful, and all worth keeping. To the artist, new experiences of "truth" are new incentives to the game, new possibilities of expression, no more. He believes in them, he takes them seriously, just so far as he needs to in order to give them the fullest and profoundest expression. In all that he is very serious, serious even to tears—but yet *not quite*—and by consequence, not at all. His artistic seriousness is of an absolute nature, it is "dead-earnest playing." But his intellectual seriousness is not absolute, it is only serious for the purposes of the game. Among comrades the artist is so ready to mock at his own seriousness, that Wagner could actually send the *Parsifal* text to Nietzsche with the signature: "R. Wagner, Member of the Consistory." But Nietzsche was no comrade. Such good-natured toleration could not soften the sour and deadly, the absolute seriousness of his feeling against the Popish Christianity of a production—of which, however, he does say that it is the highest sort of challenge to music. When Wagner, in a childish fury, threw a Brahms score down from the piano, the spectacle of such jealous desire for single domination made Nietzsche sad; he said, "At that moment Wagner was not great." If Wagner by way of relaxation talked nonsense and told Saxon jokes, Nietzsche blushed for him. I can understand Nietzsche's embarrassment at this alacrity in moving from one plane to another; but something in me—perhaps fellow-feeling with Wagner as an artist—warns me not to understand it too well.

His acquaintance with the philosophy of Arthur Schopenhauer was the greatest event in Wagner's life. No earlier intellectual contact, such as that with Feuerbach, approaches it in personal and historical significance. It meant to him the deepest consolation, the highest self-confirmation; it meant release of mind and spirit, it was utterly and entirely pertinent. There is no doubt that it freed his music from bondage and gave it courage to be itself. Wagner had little faith in the reality of friendship. In his eyes, and according to his experience, the barriers of personality separating one soul from another make solitude inevitable, and full understanding an impossibility. Here he felt himself understood, and he understood completely. "My friend Schopenhauer"; "A gift from heaven to my loneliness." "But one friend I have," he writes, "whom I love ever to win anew. That is my old Schopenhauer, who seems so grumpy and is always so deeply loving." "When I have urged my feelings to their utmost, what a joy and refreshment to open that book and suddenly find myself again, to see myself so well understood and clearly expressed, only in quite a different language, which suffering quickly makes me understand . . . that is a wonderful and gratifying reciprocal effect, and ever new because ever stronger. . . . How beautiful, that the old man knows nothing of what he is to me, and *what I am to myself through him.*"

A piece of good luck like this, among artists, is only possible where they speak different languages; otherwise catastrophe and deadly rivalry ensue. But where the medium of one is thought, of the other form, all jealousy engendered by the similarity or proximity of mental states is obviated. The *pereant qui ante nos nostra dixerunt* has no bearing, nor has Goethe's question: "Does one live, then, when others live?" On the contrary, the very fact of the other's existence means help at need, it means unexpected and blessed clarifying and strengthening of one's own being. Never probably in the history of the mind has there been so wonderful an example of the artist, the dark and driven human being, finding spiritual support, self-justification and enlightenment in another's thought, as in this case of Wagner and Schopenhauer.

The World as Will and Idea : what memories of one's own young intoxications of the spirit, one's own joys of conception, compact of melancholy and gratitude, come up at the thought of the bond between Wagner's work and this great book ! This comprehensive critique and guide, this poesy of knowledge, this metaphysics of impulse and spirit, will and idea as conceived by the artist, this marvellous thought-structure of ethical, pessimistical and musical elements—what profound, epoch-making, human affinities it displays with the score of the *Tristan* ! The old words come back, in which the stripling described the Schopenhauer experience of his bourgeois hero : "He was filled with a great, surpassing satisfaction. It soothed him to see how a master-mind could lay hold on this strong, cruel, mocking thing called life and enforce it and condemn it. His was the gratification of the sufferer who has always had a bad conscience about his sufferings and concealed them from the gaze of a harsh, unsympathetic world, until suddenly, from the hand of an authority, he receives, as it were, justification and licence for his suffering—justification before the world, this best of all possible worlds which the master-mind scornfully demonstrates to be the worst of all possible ones." They come back, these old phrases of gratitude and homage that still express so well the tremulous rapture of the past—and of the present: that rousing out of brief and heavy sleep, that sudden and exquisitely startling awakening, to find in one's own heart the seed of a metaphysic which proves the ego to be illusion, death a release from that ego's insufficiency; the world a product of the will, and his own eternal possession, so long as he does not deny himself in knowledge, but finds his way from vanity to peace. That is the conclusion, the doctrine of wisdom and salvation subjoined to a philosophy of the will which has little to do with the wisdom of peace and rest, being a conception which could only have its source in a nature tormented by will and impulse; in which, indeed, the impulse to clarification, spiritualisation and knowledge was just as strong as the other sinister urgency; the conception of a universal eros which expressly considers sex to be the focus of the will, and the æsthetic point of view, as that of pure and disinterested contemplation, the only and primary possibility of release from the torture of instinct. Out of the will, out of desire contrary to better knowledge, this philosophy, which is the will's intellectual denial, is born; and thus it was that Wagner, whose nature was profoundly akin to the philosopher's own, felt it and seized upon it with the greatest gratitude, as something essentially his own and answering to his needs. For his nature too was combined of urgent and tormenting desires for power and pleasure, together with longings for moral enlightenment and release; it was a conflict of passion and desire for peace. And thus a system of thought which is an extraordinary mixture of quietism and heroics, which calls "happiness" a chimera, and gives out that the highest and best we can attain to is a life of heroic struggle—must have rejoiced a nature like Wagner's, must have seemed made to fit him and created for him.

The official works on Wagner assert in all seriousness that *Tristan* was not influenced by the Schopenhauerian philosophy. That seems to me a curious lack of insight. The arch-romantic worship of the night embodied in this sublimely morbid, consuming, enchanting work, deep-dyed in all the worst and highest mysteries of the romantic essence, has about it nothing specifically Schopenhauerian. The sensuous, super-sensuous intuitions in the *Tristan* come from a remoter source: from the perfervid and hectic Novalis, who writes: "Union joined not only for life but for death is a marriage that gives us a companion for the night. Love is sweetest in death; for the living death is a bridal night, a sweet mysterious secret." And in the *Hymns to Night* he complains: "Must morning always come? Does the domain of the earthly never cease? Will it never be that love's sweet sacrifice shall burn for ever on the altar?" Tristan and Isolde call themselves the "Night-consecrate"—the phrase actually occurs in Novalis: "Consecrated to the night." And still more striking from the point of view of literary history, still more significant for the sources of *Tristan*, for its emotional and intellectual bases, are its associations with a little book of evil repute, I mean Friedrich von Schlegel's *Lucinde*. I quote a passage from this work: "We are immortal as love. I can no longer say my love or thy love, both being so utterly one, love as much given as returned. It is marriage, eternal union and bond between our spirits, not alone for what we call this world, but for a true, indivisible, nameless, infinite world, for our whole, everlasting life and being." Here is the mental image of the love- and death-potion: "Thus I too, if the time seemed come, would drain a cup of laurel-water with thee, freely and gladly, as the last glass of champagne we drank together, with the words, 'Let us drink out the rest of our lives!' " And here is the thought of the *Liebestod*: "I know you too would not outlive me, you would follow to the grave your impatient spouse, from love and longing you would descend into the flaming abyss whither the Indian woman is driven by a desperate law, which by harsh and deliberate enforcement violates and destroys the most delicate sanctuaries of the free will." And there is a reference to the "Exaltation of voluptuousness," surely a very Wagnerian formula. Here indeed is an erotic, mystical prose poem, in praise and adoration of sleep, the paradise of rest, the holy silence of passivity, which in *Tristan* becomes the lulling motif of the horns and the divided violins. And it was nothing less than a literary discovery that I made, when as a young man I underlined the ecstatic passage between Julian and Lucinde: "O eternal yearning! For the fruitless desire and vain brilliance of the day die down and expire, and a great night of love knows eternal repose," and wrote in the margin: "*Tristan.*" To this day I do not know whether anyone has ever remarked this case of unconscious verbal memory and imitation, as little as I know whether scholars are aware that Nietzsche took from *Lucinde* his title for the book he calls *Fröhliche Wissenschaft* ("Joyous Wisdom").

Its cult of the night, its execration of the day, are what stamps the *Tristan* as romantic, as fundamentally affiliated with all the romantic aspects of emotion and thought—and as such not needing the Schopenhauerian sign-manual. Night is the kingdom and home of all romanticism, her own discovery, always she has played it off against the empty vanities of the day, as the kingdom of the sensibilities against reason. I shall never forget the impression made upon me by Linderhof, the castle of the ailing and beauty-consumed King Ludwig; for I saw there the preponderance of the night expressed in the very proportions of the rooms. This little pleasure palace situated in the wonderful mountain solitudes has rather small and insignificant living-rooms, and only one room of relative magnificence of size and decoration: the sleeping-chamber. It is full of the heavy splendour of gilding and silk, its state bed lies under a canopy and is flanked by gold candelabra. Here is the true state apartment of the royal chalet, and it is dedicated to the night. This deliberate stress upon the night, the lovelier half of the day, is arch-romantic; and its romanticism is bound up with the whole mother- and moon-cult which since the dawn of human time and human sun-worship has stood opposed to the male and father-religion of the light. Wagner's *Tristan* belongs, generally speaking, to this world.

But when the Wagner authorities say that *Tristan* is a love-drama, as such contains the strongest affirmation of the will to live, and in consequence has nothing to do with Schopenhauer; when they insist that the night therein celebrated is the night of love "*wo Liebeswonne uns lacht*," and that if this drama has a philosophy at all then it is the exact opposite of the doctrine which would deny the will, and that precisely on that ground it is independent of the Schopenhauerian metaphysics—it seems to me that all this betrays a strange psychological insensitiveness. The denial of the will is the moral and intellectual content of Schopenhauer's philosophy, of secondary significance and not the crucial point. His philosophic system is fundamentally erotic in its nature, and in so far as it is that the *Tristan* is saturated with it. The quenching of the torch in the second act of the mystery play is emphasised in the orchestra by the death motif, the lovers' cry of transport, "*Selbst dann bin ich die Welt*," with the longing motif out of the depths of the psychological and mythical accompanying music—is that not Schopenhauer? Wagner is mythological poet not less in *Tristan* than in the *Ring*; even the love drama deals with a myth of the origin of the world. "Often," so he writes from Paris in 1860, to Mathilde Wesendonck, "I look with yearning toward the land of Nirvana. But Nirvana soon becomes *Tristan* again. You know the story of the Buddhistic theory of the origin of the world? A breath troubles the clearness of the heavens"—he writes the four chromatic ascending notes with which his *opus metaphysicum* begins and ends, the *g*-sharp, *a*, *a*-sharp, *b*-natural—"it swells and condenses, and there before me is the whole vast solid mass of the world." It is the symbolic tone-thought which we know as the "*Sehnsuchtsmotif*," and which in the cosmogony of the *Tristan* signifies the beginning of all things, like the E-major of the Rhine motif in the *Ring*. It is Schopenhauer's "will," represented by what Schopenhauer called the "focus of the will,' the yearning for love. And this mythical equating of sexual desire with the sweet and fatal world-creating principle that first troubled the clear heaven of the inane—that is so Schopenhauerian that the refusal of the experts to see it looks like obstinacy.

"How could we die," asks Tristan, in the early, not yet versified draft; "what would there be of us to kill, that would not be love? Are we not utterly and only love? Can our love ever end? Could I ever will to love, love no more? Were I now to die would love die too, since we are naught but love?" The quotation shows the unhesitating equation of love and will on the part of the poet. The latter stands simply for the love of life, which cannot end in death, though it is freed from the fetters of individuality. Most interesting it is too to see the love-mythus sustained as a conception of the drama and preserved from any historical or religious clouding or distortion. Phrases like "Whether bound for hell or heaven," surviving in the draft, are omitted from the production. We have here doubtless a conscious weakening of the historical element, but it is limited to the intellectual and philosophical and only happens in the interest of these. And it suits admirably with a most intensive technique of coloration, applied to the landscape settings, the cultural elements, the racial characteristics of the protagonists. It is stylistic specialisation of in-incredible ability and certainty of touch. Nowhere does Wagner's skill at mimicry triumph more magically than in the style of the *Tristan*—this not as a matter of language merely, by phraseology in the spirit of the court epic; for with intuitive genius he is able to saturate his word and tone painting in an Anglo-Norman-French atmosphere, with a discernment which shows how completely the Wagner soul is at home in the pre-national sphere of European life. The divorce from history, the free humanisation, takes place only in the field of speculative thought, and then in the service of the erotic myth. For its sake heaven and hell are cut out. Christianity too, since it would amount to historical atmosphere. There is no God, no one knows Him or calls upon Him. There is nothing but erotic philosophy, atheistic metaphysics : the cosmogonic myth in which the *Sehnsuchtsmotif* evokes the world.

Wagner's good normal way of being ill, his rather morbid way of being heroic, are simply indications of the contradictions and cross-currents in his nature, its duality and manifoldness, as manifested in such apparently contradictory elements as the psychological and mythological bents to which I have already referred. To call him romantic is still probably the most apt characterisation of his nature ; but the concept romantic is itself so complex and changeable that it seems to be less a category than the abandonment of categories.

Only in the romantic can popular appeal unite with the extreme of subtlety, with a "heinous self-indulgence" in means and effects—and it alone can make possible that "double optic" of which Nietzsche speaks with reference to Wagner : that knows how to cater to the coarsest and the finest—unconsciously, of course, for it would be stupid to introduce the element of calculation—whose *Lohengrin* can enrapture spirits like the author of the *Fleurs du Mal* and at the same time serve to elevate the masses ;

that leads a Kundryish double life as a Sunday afternoon opera and as the idol of initiate and suffering and supersensitive souls. The romantic—in league, of course, with music, toward which it continually aspires, without which it can have no fulfilment—knows no exclusiveness, no "pathos of distance"; it says to nobody: "This is not for you"; one side of its nature stands with the least and lowest, and let nobody say that is the case with all great art. Great art may elsewhere too have succeeded in uniting the childlike and the elevated; but the combination of the extremely *raffiné* with fairy-story simplicity, the power to materialise—and popularise—the highly intellectual under the guise of an orgy of the senses; the ability to make the essentially grotesque put on the garment of consecration, the Last Supper, the bell, the elevation of the Host . . . to couple sex and religion in an opera of greatly daring sex-appeal, and to set up that sort of holy-unholy artistic establishment in the middle of Europe as a kind of Lourdes theatre and miraculous grotto for the voracious credulity of a decadent world—all that is nothing but romantic. In the classic and humanistic, the really high sphere of art, it is quite unthinkable. Take the list of characters in *Parsifal*: what a set! One advanced and offensive degenerate after another: a self-castrated magician; a desperate double personality, composed of a vamp and a repentant Magdalene, with cataleptic transition stages; a love-sick high-priest, awaiting the redemption which is to come to him in the person of a chaste youth ; the youth himself, "pure" fool and redeemer, quite a different figure from Brunnhilde's lively awakener and in his way also an extremely rare specimen—they are like the aggregation of scarecrows in A. von Arnim's famous coach that travelled from Brake to Brussels : the captivating gipsy witch who is really nothing but an old hag ; the good-for-nothing, who is a corpse ; the spectre who behaves like a fascinating woman ; and the Field-Marshal Cornelius Nepos, who is a slip of mandrake grown beneath the gallows, where, as Heine says, the most dissembling tears of a hanged man have flowed. The comparison sounds blasphemous ; and yet the solemn personages in *Parsifal* have the same flavour of romantic extravaganza, they spring from the same school of taste as do von Arnim's disreputable crew, though the fact would be more obvious if the literary form were fiction instead of drama. As it is, the music shrouds it from view in consecration and mythology ; it is music's power over the emotions that makes the ensemble appear not like a half-burlesque, half-uncanny impropriety of the romantic school, but as a miracle play of the highest religious significance.

Youth is typically susceptible to this elusive problem of art and the essence of the artist, it has a melancholy understanding of the ironic interplay of nature and effect ; in this field I recall many an utterance of my own young days, characteristic of the Wagner passion that has gone through the fire of the Nietzschean critique, dictated by that "disgust of knowledge"—which is the foremost and peculiar lesson youth learns therefrom. Nietzsche said he would not touch the *Tristan* score with the tongs. "Who will dare," he cries, "to utter the word, the right word for the *ardeurs* of the *Tristan*-music ?" I am more open to the rather comic old-maidishness of this question than I was when I was twenty-five years old. For what is there so venturesome about it ? Sensuality, enormous sensuality, mounting into the mythical, spiritualised, depicted with the extreme of naturalism, sensuality unquenchable by any amount of gratification—that is the "word." And one asks, whence comes the violent bitterness against sex that expresses itself in such a psychological denunciation in the question of Nietzsche, the "free, very free spirit." Is not this Nietzsche the arch-moralist and clergyman's son ? And what has become of his rôle as defender of life against morality ? He applies to the *Tristan* the mystic's formula : voluptuous pleasure of hell ("*Wollust der Hölle*"). Good. And one need only compare the mysticism of the *Tristan* with that of Goethe's "blessed longing" and its "higher mating" to feel how little we are in the Goethe sphere. But Nietzsche himself is after all no poorer an instance than Wagner of the fact that the soul-state of the Western world in the nineteenth century has deteriorated by comparison with Goethe's epoch. And the sort of lashing to fury or drugging to calm which are among Wagner's effects

—the ocean too can show the same, and nobody thinks of dragging its psychology to the light of day. What is allowed to great nature should be allowed to great art ; when Baudelaire, in naive artistic rapture, and quite without moral prejudice, speaks of the "ecstasy of bliss and understanding" which the *Lohengrin* overture put him in, and raves of the "opium intoxication," of the "desire that in high places circles" he shows much more courage and intellectual freedom than Nietzsche with his suspicious caution. Though after all the phrase in which Nietzsche characterises the Wagner craze as "a slight unconscious epidemic of sensuality" still has its justification, and it is precisely the word "unconscious" which, in view of Wagner's romantic popularity, may irritate such as feel the need of clear thinking ; may be a ground for "preferring not to be there."

Wagner's power of concentrating the intellectual and the popular in a single dramatic figure, is nowhere better displayed than in the hero of his revolutionary phase—in Siegfried. The "breathless delight" with which the future Director of the Bayreuth Theatre one day witnessed a puppet show —he tells about it in his essay on Actors and Singers —bore practical fruit in the setting of the *Ring*, which is an ideal popular diversion with just the right kind of go-ahead hero. Who can fail to recognise in him the little whip-cracker of the county fair? But at the same time he is a northern sun-myth and god of light—which does not prevent him from being something modern too, out of the nineteenth century, the free man, the breaker of tablets and renovator of a fallen society: Bakunin, in short, as Bernard Shaw, with cheerful rationalism, quite simply calls him. Yes, he is a clown, a sun-god and an anarchistic social revolutionary, all rolled into one, what more can the theatre demand? And this art of combination is simply an expression of Wagner's own mingled and manifold nature. He is not musician and not poet, but a third category, in which the other two are blended in a way unknown before; he is a theatre-Dionysius, who knows how to take unprecedented methods of expression and give them a poetic basis, to a certain extent to rationalise them. But in so far as he *is* poet, it is not in a modern, literary and cultivated spirit, not out of his mind and consciously, but in a much deeper and devouter way. It is the folk-soul that speaks out of him and through him; he is only its tool and mouthpiece, only "God's ventriloquist" to repeat Nietzsche's good joke. At least, this is the correct and accepted theory of his artistic position, and it is supported by a kind of unwieldy awkwardness which his work betrays when considered as literature. And yet he can write: "We should not underestimate the power of reflection; the unconsciously produced work of art belongs to periods remote from ours, and the art product of the most highly cultivated period cannot be produced otherwise than in full consciousness." That is a blow between the eyes for the theory which would ascribe an entirely mythical origin to his works; and indeed, though these indubitably bear in part the marks of inspiration, of blind and blissful ecstasy, yet there is so much else, so much cleverness, wittiness, allusiveness, calculated effect; so much dwarfish industry accompanies the labours of gods and giants, that it is impossible to believe in trance and mystery. The extraordinary understanding displayed in his abstract writings, does not indeed act in the service of spirit, truth, abstract knowledge; but to the advantage of his work, which it labours to explain and justify, whose pathway it would smooth, both within and without. But it is none the less a fact. And there would remain the possibility that in the act of creation he was entirely shoved aside to make room for the promptings of the folk-soul. But my feeling of the improbability of this is strengthened by various more or less well-authenticated statements from those who knew him, to the effect that by his own account some of his best things were produced by dint of sheer hard thinking. "Ah, how I have tried and tried," he is reported as saying, "thought and thought, until at last I get hold of what I wanted."

In short, his author- and creatorship has contact with both spheres: the one which lies "remote from ours" as well as the one where the brain long ago developed into the modern intellectual tool we know.

And hence the indissoluble mingling of the dæmonic and the bourgeois which is the essence of him. Much the same is true of Schopenhauer, who is accordingly Wagner's next of kin, both in time and in temperament. The unbourgeois extravagance of his nature, which he himself laid at the door of music ("it makes a purely exclamatory man of me," says he ; "the note of exclamation is the only satisfying punctuation to me so soon as I leave my notes"), this extravagance finds expression in the exaggerated character of all his moods, particularly the depressive. It comes out in the strange destinies of his outer life—destiny being nothing more than the unfolding of character —his wryness *vis-à-vis* the world, his hunted, outlawed, broken and battered existence ; he puts it in the mouth of his *Wehwalt* Siegmund :

"Drew I to men or to women,
Many I met, where I them found,
If I for friend, for woman wooed,
Ever still was I despisèd,
Curses lay upon me.
What right ever I called
Still to them seemèd it wrong ;
What to me evil appear'd
Others counted it right.
Fell I on feud, whither I went ;
Where I me found, scorn met me.
Long'd I for bliss, waked I to woe."

Every word comes from experience ; not one but is coined out of his own life ; in these fine lines there is no more than he wrote in prose to Mathilde Wesendonck : "Since the world, in all seriousness, does not want me"—or to her husband : "I am so hard to accommodate in this world, that a thousand misunderstandings are always likely to take place. This is my great trouble . . . the world and I knock our heads together and the thinnest skull gets split—no wonder I have my nervous headaches." The desperate humour of this is quite in character. Once, round his forty-eighth birthday, he speaks of the "crazy mood" he was in, in Weimar; it delighted everybody, but originated solely in the circumstance that he did not dare be serious, simply did not dare any more, for fear of going to pieces. "This is a fault of my temperament, and it gets worse and worse. I fight against it, for sometimes it seems to me I shall weep myself away." What a luxury of debility! What *Kapellmeister Kreisler* eccentricity! All this passionate up and down, this frenzied and tragic emotionalism, reduced to its starkest elements, accursed, yet pining for rest and peace, he has concentrated in the figure of the Flying Dutchman; it lives and glows with the colours of his own anguish; the great intervals in which the score of this rôle swings to and fro, are most calculated to create this impression of wild agitation.

No, this is no bourgeois—at least not in any sense of being adaptable or conformable to rule. And yet he has the atmosphere of the bourgeoisie, the atmosphere of his century, about him, as has Schopenhauer the capitalist philosopher: the moral pessimism, the mood of decline set to music—that is genuine nineteenth century, and goes with its tendency to the monumental, its penchant for size—as though size were a property of morality. He has, I say, the atmosphere of the bourgeois, and not only in this general sense but in one much more personal. I will not insist that he was a revolutionary of the '48, a fighter for the middle-class and thus a political citizen. For he was that only in his own peculiar way, as an artist and in the interest of his art, which was revolutionary and might hope for imagined advantages, better conditions and more effectiveness from an upset of the existing order. But there are more intimate traits of character—despite its genius and its inspiration—which distinctly suggest the bourgeois attitude. As when he moved into that asylum on the green hill near Zürich and in the enjoyment of his sense of well-being wrote to Liszt: "Everything is arranged for permanence and convenience, and precisely as one would wish; everything is just in the right place. My study has the same fastidious air of comfort and elegance that is familiar to you; the desk stands by the big window. . . ." The fastidious order and also the bourgeois elegance he requires of his surroundings correspond to the element of shrewd and calculated industry which accompanies inspiration in his work, and supplies the bourgeois flavour of it. His later self-dramatisation as *Deutscher Meister* with the black velvet cap had its good inward and natural justification; despite all volcanic manifestations it would be a mistake to overlook the old-German element, the loyal-eyed, industrious and ingenious artisan which is just as essential to it. He writes to Otto Wesendonck: "Let me tell you briefly the state of my work. When I began it I abandoned hope of being able to bring it to a conclusion in short order. . . . Partly because I was so full of cares and troubles of all sorts that I was often incapable of production. But partly also because I soon discovered my peculiar relation to my present work (which now I simply cannot do in a hurry, but can find pleasure therein only because I owe to good ideas that come to me even the smallest detail in it and work it out accordingly). I see this so clearly and unchangeably that I am obliged to give up any hasty or incomplete work which alone would enable me to finish in time." That is the "uprightness and good faith" which Schopenhauer inherited from his merchant forbears and which he claimed to have carried over into realms of the mind. It means solid, painstaking, accurate labour, and it shows itself in the scores: they are clean, careful work, nothing slovenly about them—even that product of transport, the *Tristan*, is a model of clear, painstaking calligraphy.

But it cannot be denied that Wagner's taste for bourgeois elegance has its degenerate side; it betrays the tendency to put on a character which is quite remote from the sixteenth-century German *Meister* in the Dürer cap; it is bad nineteenth century, it *is* bourgeois. The smack of the modern middle-class (as distinct from the old civic spirit) is there, unmistakably in his human and artistic personality: all this luxury and extravagance, this silk and satin and "*Gründerzeit*" grandeur; it is of course a trait of his private life, but the roots of it go deep down. It is the time, and the taste of the Makart bouquet with the peacock feathers which used to adorn the gilt and upholstered salons of the bourgeoisie; the fact is known that Wagner had the idea of engaging Makart to paint his scenery. He writes to Frau Ritter: "I've been having for some time now another craze for luxury (*ein Narr an Luxus*); whoever knew what it has to take the place of for me would consider me very modest indeed. Every morning I sit down and work in the midst of it; it is absolute necessity to me, for a day without work is torture." It would be hard to say which is more bourgeois, the love of luxury, or the torture felt at a day without work. But it is at this point that we discover the bourgeois striking back again into the disordered and unsavoury realms of art, and taking on a character which, morbid as it is, has something dignified and even touching about it; something to which the word bourgeois is quite inapplicable. Here we enter a different field altogether, the fantastic domain of *stimulation*—Wagner treats of it, with restraint and circumlocution, in a letter to Liszt: "It is actually only with the most genuine despair that I take up my art again. If this must happen, if I must once more resign reality and plunge into that sea of fantasy, then at least my imagination must get help and support from somewhere. I cannot live like a dog, I cannot sleep on straw and drink bad brandy. I must be soothed and flattered in my soul, if I am to succeed at this gruelling job of creating a world out of nothing. In order to take up the plan of the *Ring* again and envisage its actual performance, there had to be all sorts of contributing factors to give me the necessary atmosphere of art and luxury. I *had* to be able to live better than I have done in the past!" His "*Narr an Luxus*" is well known, the technique that had to come to the help of his fancy: the wadded silk dressing-gowns, the lace-trimmed satin bed-covers embroidered with garlands of roses, these are the palpable expressions of an extravagance of taste for which he ran up debts in thousands. Arrayed in them he sits down mornings to the gruelling job, by dint of them he achieves the "atmosphere of luxury and art" necessary to the creation of primitive Nordic heroes and exalted natural symbolism, to the conception of his sun-blond youthful hero striking sparks from the anvil as he forges his victorious sword—all which goes to swell the breast of German youth with lofty feelings of manly glory.

In reality the contradiction is without significance. Who thinks of Schiller's rotten apples—the smell of which used to make Goethe nearly faint—as an argument against the lofty sincerity of his works? Wagner's working conditions happen to come higher than Schiller's—and it would not be hard to think of costumes (for instance, dressing up as a soldier or a monk) more suitable than satin dressing-gowns to the stern service of art. But in both cases we are dealing with an artist pathology, harmless even though a bit uncanny; only Philistines would be misled by it. Yet after all there is some difference between the two. In all Schiller's work there is no trace of the odour of decay which stimulated his brain; but who would deny that there is a suggestion of satin dressing-gowns in Wagner's art? True it is, that Schiller's purposeful idealism realises itself much more purely and unequivocally in the influence his works exert, than Wagner's ethical attitude does in his. He was zealous for reform in a cultural sense, he was against art as a luxury, against luxury in art; he wanted the purification and spiritualisation of the operatic theatre—which he conceived of as synonymous with art. He referred with contempt to Rossini as "Italia's voluptuous son, smiling away in luxury's most luxurious lap"; he spoke of the Italian opera as a "daughter of joy," of the French as a "cold-smiling coquette." But his ethical attitude as artist, the hatred and hostility these phrases suggest, does not find very happy expression in either the meaning or the method of his own art, which brought the bourgeois society of all Europe to bow beneath its spell. What was it drove these thousands into the arms of his art—what, but the blissfully sensuous, searing, sense-consuming, intoxicating, hypnotically caressing, heavily upholstered—in a word, the luxurious quality of his music? Eichendorff's song of the bold young bachelors, one of whom wastes his life in evil dissipations, characterises temptation as "the wantoning waves," as "the billows' bright maw." Wonderful. None but a romantic could so suggestively characterise sin—and Wagner, in *Tannhäuser* and *Parsifal*, has done as much. And Wagner's orchestra, is it not just such a "bright maw" out of which, like Eichendorff's young Fant, one wakens "weary and old"?

If we must, in part, answer in the affirmative such questions as these, we are bound at the same time to recognise that we are dealing with what one calls a tragic antinomy, with one of the involved contradictions and incongruities in Wagner's nature. There are many of these, and a good part of them have to do with the relation between intention and effect in art; therefore it is highly important to emphasise here the complete and honourable purity and idealism of Wagner's position as artist, in order to obviate all possible misunderstandings on the score of the mass-success his art achieved. All criticism, even Nietzsche's, tends to attribute the effectiveness of art to a conscious and deliberate intention of the artist, and to suggest calculation. Quite falsely and mistakenly: as though every artist does not do just what he *is*, what seems good and beautiful to *him*; as though there could be a kind of artist, to whom his own effectiveness was a sham, instead of being, as it always is, an effect first of all upon him, the artist himself! Innocent may be the last adjective to apply to art; but the artist, he is innocent. An enormous success, such as that which Wagner's theatre of music "aimed at," was never before vouchsafed to great art. It is fifty years since the master's death; and every evening this music envelops the globe. This art of the theatre, this art of shaking the masses, owns such elements—imperialistic, world-subduing, despotic, powerfully *agaçante*, inflammable, demagogic elements—as to make one deduce a monstrous ambition, a Caesar's will to power as the force that set them in motion. The truth looks different. "So much I tell you," Wagner writes from Paris to his beloved. "Only the conviction of my own purity gives me this power. I feel myself pure: I know in my deepest soul that I always worked for others, never for myself; and my constant sufferings are a proof to me." If that is not true, it is at least so sincere that scepticism is silenced. He knows naught of ambition. "Of greatness, fame, conquest of the masses," he assures Liszt, "I think nothing." Not even conquest of the masses? Perhaps, in the mild form of popularity, as ideal, wish-dream, as the romantic, democratic conception of art and artists, which the *Meistersinger* so sturdily and splendidly embodies. Yes, the popularity of Hans Sachs, against whom the whole school labours in vain because the people worship him—that is a wish-dream. In the *Meistersinger* there is a coquetting with the folk as in the character of final arbiter of art, which is the opposite of the aristocratic position and highly indicative of Wagner's democratic revolutionarism in art, his conception of it as a free appeal to the feeling of the people. What a contrast to the classic, courtly and elegant notion of art obtaining in that time when Voltaire wrote: "*Quand la populace se mêle de raisonner*, *tout est perdu*." And still, when this artist reads Plutarch, he feels, unlike Karl Moor, dislike of the "great men," and would not be like them for anything. "Hateful, violent, greedy little natures—because they have nothing in themselves and must always be sucking it in from outside. Away with your great men! I agree with Schopenhauer: not he who conquers, but he who overcomes the world, is worthy of admiration. God save me from these Napoleons!" Was he a world-conqueror, or a world-overcomer? And his "*Selbst dann bin ich die Welt*," with its world-erotic theme and accent—of which of the two is that the formula?

In any case, the charge of ambition in the ordinary worldly sense is not tenable; because he worked at first without hope of immediate results, without any prospect of them under the actually existing circumstances and conditions. Worked in the void of fancy, as it were, for an imaginary ideal stage, the realisation of which, for the time, was not to be thought of. Certainly there is no talk of shrewd calculation and ambitious exploitation of possibilities in the letter he writes to Otto Wesendonck: "For this I see: I am only wholly what I am, when I create. The performance of my works belongs to a purer time—a time which I must first prepare for by my sufferings. My closest friends have only astonishment for my new labours: no one who has relations with our official art-life feels strength to hope. And they are right. Nothing shows me better how far ahead I am of everything round me." The loneliness of genius, its remoteness from actuality, has never been more arrestingly expressed, than in these words. But we—we of the last decade of the nineteenth century and the first third of the twentieth, of the world war and the slow decline of capitalism; we in whose day Wagner's art bestrides the theatres of the civilised world and triumphs everywhere in unabridged performances—we are those "purer times" which he had to prepare through his sufferings? Is the humanity of from 1880 to 1933 the one to prove the height and goodness of an art by the giant success we have vouchsafed it?

Let us not ask. We see how his genius proves itself by the fact that it seeks to come near the world, to adapt itself to the world—and cannot. A comic operetta, a satyr-play to the *Tannhäuser*, a diversion for him and his audience; the best of wills to create something light and enjoyable—it turns out to be the *Meistersinger*. Well, then, something Italian, something tuneful, lyrical and singable, with a small caste, easy to produce, quite simple:

and the result is—*Tristan.* One cannot make oneself smaller than one is : one does what one is, and art is truth—the truth about the artist.

Yes, the vast universal effectiveness of this art had, originally and personally speaking, very pure and spiritual sources. This was first of all due to its own lofty plane, where no deeper scorn is known than that for effect, for "effect without cause." And next because all the imperial, demagogic and mass-effective elements must be conceived in a quite ultra-practical and ideal sense as having reference to all too revolutionary conditions yet to be achieved. In particular the innocence of the artist comes in play, where the will to rouse enthusiasm expresses itself, powerfully instrumented, in a national appeal, celebrating and glorifying the German spirit, as happens quite directly in *Lohengrin*, in King Henry's "German Sword" and in the *Meistersinger* on the honest lips of good Hans Sachs. It is thoroughly inadmissible to ascribe to Wagner's nationalistic attitudes and speeches the meaning they would have to-day. That would be to falsify and misuse them, to besmirch their romantic purity.

The national idea, when Wagner introduced it as a familiar and workable theme into his works, that is to say, before it was realised, was in its heroic, historically legitimate epoch. It had its good, living and genuine period ; it was poetry and intellect, a future value. But when the basses thunder out at the stalls the verse from the "German Sword," or that kernel and finale of the *Meistersinger* :

> "Though Holy Roman Empire sink to dust
> There still survives our sacred German art"

in order to arouse an ulterior patriotic emotion—that is demagogy. It is precisely these lines—they already appeared at the end of the first sketch, dated Marienbad, 1845—that attest the intellectuality of Wagner's nationalism and its remoteness from the political sphere ; they betray a complete anarchistic indifference to the state, so long as the spiritually German, the "*Deutsche Kunst*," survives. Even so he was not thinking of German art, but rather of his music-theatre, which is far from being solely German, having taken unto itself not only Weber, Marschner and Lortzing, but also Spontini and Grand Opera—but that is another matter. At bottom perhaps he thought, like that greatest unpatriot of them all, Goethe : "What do the Germans want ? Have they not me ?"

All his life long, Richard Wagner dreamed of an ideal public for his art, in the sense of a classless society, founded on love, freed from luxury and the curse of gold ; thus as a politician he was much more of a Socialist, a believer in a cultural utopia, than he was a patriot in the sense of the all-powerful state. His heart was for the poor against the rich. His participation in the '48 cost him twelve years of torment and exile ; later, repenting of his "abandoned" optimism, in face of the *fait accompli* of Bismarck's empire, he minimised his share in it and identified it as best he could with the realisation of his dream. He went the way of the German bourgeoisie: from the revolution to disillusionment, to pessimism and a sheltered and contemplative resignation. And yet we find in his writings the opinion—in a certain sense the very un-German opinion: "Whoever tries to get away from the political befools himself!" So living and radical a spirit was of course aware of the unity of the problem for humanity, of the inseparability of mind and politics; he did not cling to the delusion of the German citizen, that one may be a man of culture yet not of politics—this madness to which Germany owes her misery. His attitude toward the Fatherland, from the founding of the empire to his settling down in Bayreuth, was always that of the solitary; misunderstood, repulsed, full of scorn and criticism. "Oh, how full of enthusiasm I am for the German league of the Germanic nation!" he writes from Lucerne in 1859. "God forbid that that reprobate of a Louis Napoleon should lay his hands on my dear German league: I should feel too upset if anything were to alter there!" In exile he was consumed with longing for Germany; but the return brought him nothing but bitter disappointment. "It is a miserable country," he cries, "and it is a just judgment that says the German is mean-spirited." But observe: these unfavourable comments refer solely to the German unreadiness to accept his work ; their animus is quite childish and personal. Germany is good, or bad, according as it has faith in him or denies it to him. Even in 1875 he replies to a flattering remark that the German public had surrendered to him to a most unexampled extent, with the bitter comment : "Oh, yes, the Sultan and the Khedive have taken patrons' tickets."

It is an honour to his artist heart that at the same time he could envisage the fulfilment of his German desires in the foundation of the empire by Bismarck, the new empire for which Nietzsche could not find enough words of passionate execration ; that he was ready and able to see in it the right soil for his cultural labours. The—little German—resurrection of the German Empire, a phenomenon of overpowering historical success, strengthened in Wagner, his friend Heckel says, a belief in the development of a German culture and art—in other words, the possibility that his artistic contribution, the sublimated opera, might be realised. It was this hope that gave rise to the *Kaisermarsch* ; to the poem to the German army before Paris, which only shows that without music Wagner is no poet ; to the incredibly bad taste of the *Capitulation*, a satire on Paris in her agony, in 1871, which is in every sense a betrayal of Wagner's higher self. But above all it gave rise to his manifesto, "On the Production of the Festival Play : The Ring of the Nibelungs," to which he received one single reply—from friend Heckel, the piano dealer in Mannheim.

The opposition to Wagner's plans and pretensions, the fear of siding with him, remained very great; but the foundation of the empire coincided with the foundation of the first Wagner Society and the issue of patrons' cards for the festival plays. The organisation, full of compromises, as always, the realisation, was beginning. Wagner was a good enough politician to link his affairs with the Bismarck empire; he saw in it an incomparably successful feat, and he attached his own fortunes to its chariot. The European hegemony of his art has become the cultural equivalent to the political hegemony of Bismarck. The great statesman to whose labours he thus married his own, understood it not at all; he never troubled about it, he considered Wagner a crazy chap. But the old Kaiser—who understood no better—went to Bayreuth and said, "I never thought that you would bring it off!" The works of Wagner were installed as a national concern, as an official apanage of the empire; and they have remained more or less bound up with the red, white and black—however little they have to do in their deeper essence and the quality of their Germanness with all or any empires based on power and war.

When we discuss the involutions and inconsistencies of Wagner's contradictory nature, we should not leave out of account the grandiose combination and interweaving of Germanness and cosmopolitanism: it is part of his being, characterising it in the most absolutely unprecedented and thought-provoking way. There always has been, and there is to-day, a German art of high rank—I am thinking especially of the literary field—which belongs so entirely to the quiet and domestic Germany, is so peculiarly and intimately German that it is able—albeit in a very high sense—to command influence and honour only within our borders, resigning entirely all claims upon a European audience. That is a destiny like another, it has nothing to do with values. Much more insignificant stuff, the universal commonplace of the day, easily crosses the frontiers and by its very nature is everywhere understood. But other works, equal in rank and value to the exclusively domestic product, may prove to be anointed with the drop of European and democratic unction which opens the world to them and assures them international currency.

Wagner's works are of this kind—though with him one cannot speak of a drop of oil, for they fairly drip with it! Their Germanness is deep, powerful, unquestionable. The birth of drama from music, as it is consummated, purely and enchantingly, at least once, at the height of Wagner's creative powers, in the *Tristan*, could only spring out of German life; and as German in the highest sense of the word we may also characterise its tremendous sense-appeal, its mythological and metaphysical tendencies, above all, its profoundly serious consciousness as art, the high and solemn conception of the art of the theatre, with which it is filled and which it communicates.

But in and with all that, it has a universal rightness and. enjoyability above all German art of this high rank ; and I shall remain within the frame of its creator's chosen circle of thought if I reason back from the practical manifestation to the informing will. *Richard Wagner as a Cultural Phenomenon*, a book by a non-German, the Swedish Wilhelm Peterson-Berger, is very shrewd and good on this point. The writer speaks of Wagner's nationalism, of his art as a national art, and remarks that German folk-music is the only field not comprehended in the Wagnerian synthesis. In the *Meistersinger*, and in *Siegfried*, he may, for purposes of characterisation, strike the folk-key ; but it is not the fundamental note or the point of departure of his tone-poesy, from which it gushes spontaneously, as is the case with Schubert, Schumann and Brahms. It is necessary to distinguish between folk-art and national art : the first has a domestic, the second a foreign goal. Wagner's music is more national than of the people. It has many traits indeed which foreigners find German ; but it has, according to this author, an unmistakably cosmopolitan cachet.

It seems to me that this analysis of Wagner's Germanness is very finely felt and expressed. Yes, Wagner is German, he is national, in the most exemplary, perhaps too exemplary, way. For besides being an eruptive revelation of the German nature, his work is likewise a dramatic depiction of the same ; a depiction the intellectualism and the poster-like effectiveness of which is positively grotesque, positively burlesque ; it seems calculated to move an eager and palpitating world-public to the cry : "*Ah, c'est bien allemand, par exemple !*" Well, then, this Germanness, true and mighty as it is, is very modern—it is broken down and disintegrating, it is decorative, analytical, intellectual ; and hence its fascination, its inborn capacity for cosmopolitan, for world-wide effectiveness. Wagner's art is the most sensational self-portrayal and self-critique of the German nature which it is possible to conceive ; it is calculated to make Germany interesting to a foreigner even of the meanest intelligence ; and passionate preoccupation with it is at the same time passionate preoccupation with the German nature which it so decoratively criticises and glorifies. In this its nationalism consists ; but it is a nationalism so soaked in the currents of European art as to defy all effort to simplify or belittle it.

"You will serve the cause of one whom the future will hail as greatest among the great." Charles Baudelaire wrote this sentence in 1849 to a young German Wagner enthusiast and musical critic. The prophecy, astonishing in its assurance, springs from passionate love, from elective passion ; and the critical acumen of Friedrich Nietzsche is displayed in the fact that he recognised this affinity without being aware of the expression of it. "Baudelaire," he says in the studies to the *Fall Wagner*, "was once the first prophet and advocate of Delacroix ; perhaps to-day he may be the first Wagnerian in Paris." Only years later did he see the letter in which Wagner thanked the French poet for his homage—and he exulted. Yes, Baudelaire, the first admirer of Delacroix, that Wagner of the realm of painting, was actually the first Wagnerian in Paris and one of the earliest of true and passionate and artistically understanding Wagnerians. His article on *Tannhäuser*, written in 1851, was the decisive and pioneer utterance upon Wagner; it has remained historically the most important. The joy that Wagner's music gave him, the joy of finding oneself anew in the artistic conceptions of another, he had discovered in but one other case, his literary acquaintance with Edgar Allen Poe. These two, Wagner and Poe, are Baudelaire's gods—a singular juxtaposition to the German ear! It puts Wagner's art all at once in a new light; it suggests associations with which our patriotic commentators have not familiarised us. It opens up a whole world of colour and fancy, love-sick for death and beauty, the western world of high and late romanticism; a pessimistic world, adept in strange intoxicants and refinements of the senses, fanatically addicted to all sorts of æsthetical speculations and combinations; in Hoffmannian, Kreislerian dreams of the correspondence and inner relation between colours, sounds and odours, of the mystical transformations of the mingled sense. . . . In this world we are to see Richard Wagner: as the most glorious brother and comrade of all these sufferers from life, given to pity, seeking for transport, these art-mingling symbolists, worshippers of "*l'art suggestif,*" whose need it is "*d'aller au delà, plus outre que l'humanité,*" to quote Maurice Barrès, the latest convert of the cult, lover of Venice the *Tristan* city, the poet of blood, desire and death, nationalist at the end, and Wagnerian from beginning to end.

"Sind es Wellen/sanfter Lüfte ?
Sind es Wogen/wonniger Düfte ?
Wie sie schwellen, /mich umrauschen,
soll ich atmen, /soll ich lauschen ?
Soll ich schlürfen, /untertauchen,
süss in Duften/mich verhauchen ?
In des Wonnenmeeres/wogenden Schwall,
in der Duftwellen/tönenden Schall,
in des Weltatmens/wehendem All—
ertrinken— /versinken—
unbewusst— /höchste Lust !"

That is the last and highest word of the world I mean, its crown and triumph, stored and saturated with its spirit ; and it was Wagner and the early Nietzsche who conventionalised its European, mystic-sensual art into something not too impossible for German culture, and related it to the landmarks of tragedy—Euripides, Shakespeare, Beethoven. Afterwards, Nietzsche regretted his act, being irritated by a certain German lack of clarity in psychological matters ; he over-emphasised Wagner's European traits and poured scorn upon his German mastership. Wrongly. For Wagner's Germanness was strong and genuine. And that the romantic should reach its climax and achieve its universal success in German and in the guise of the German *Meister*, was determined for it beforehand, by its very nature.

A last word upon Wagner's relation to the past and to the future. For here too there reigns a duality, an interweaving of apparent contradictions, similar to the antithesis of Germanness and Europeanism which I have just analysed. There are reactionary traits in Wagner, traces of reversion and cult of the dark past; we might interpret in this sense his love of the mystical and mythological; the Protestant nationalism in the *Meistersinger* as well as the Catholic spirit in *Parsifal*; his general fondness for the Middle Ages, for the life of knights and princes, for miracles and perfervid faith. And yet my feeling for the true nature of this artist phenomenon, conditioned through and through as it was by renewal, change and liberation, strictly forbids me to take literally his language and manner of expression, instead of seeing it for what it is, an art-idiom of a very figurative sort, with which something quite different, something entirely revolutionary, keeps pace. This stormily progressive creative spirit, so charged with life despite all its soul-heaviness, its bond with death; this man who gloried in a world-destroyer born of free love; this bold musical pioneer, who in *Tristan* stands with one foot already upon a-tonal ground—to-day he would probably be called a cultural Bolshevist !—this man of the people, who all his life long and with all his heart repudiated power and money, violence and war ; whose dream of a theatre—whatever the times may have made of it—was one set up to a classless community ; such a man no retrograde spirit can claim for its own ; he belongs to that will which is directed toward the future.

But it is idle to conjure great men out of eternity into our now and here—to the end of asking them their views upon questions which were put differently in their day and thus are foreign to their spirit. How would Richard Wagner stand toward our problems, our needs and the tasks before us ? That "would" has a hollow sound, the position is unthinkable. Views are of secondary importance, even in their own present, how much more so when that has become past ! What is left is the man, and his work, the product of his efforts. Let us be content to reverence Wagner's work as a mighty and manifold phenomenon of German and Western culture, which will always act as the profoundest stimulus to art and knowledge.

GOETHE, NOVELIST

G

GOETHE, NOVELIST

(*Being an epilogue to the Epicon edition of* Elective Affinities)

THE writer admits to having had a voice in deciding which of Goethe's novels should be included in this epic pantheon. And he was sorely tempted, at first, to cast his vote for *Wilhelm Meister*. When a classical masterpiece appears in a spontaneous new edition, we get a fresh and happy sense of what it means to us as a possession; and when, as in this instance, it comes in unaffectedly modern dress, with no philological apparatus, no odour of the museum about it, so that we can look at it *de novo*, with young, unacademical eye, the masterpiece comes back as it were to life and nature, luring us to possess it anew, upon a different plane, to revalue it and make it fruitful, perhaps in undreamed-of ways, to our own economy and that of the time. To make fresh contact between the German people, at its present stage of experience and maturity, and the world of *Wilhelm Meister*—that world of pedagogic adventure, in which the cultural values ripen naturally out of the personal and narrative, and out of those in turn the social and political—here was a thought which allured the writer so strongly that he is fain to justify to himself his final choice.

The selection of *Die Wahlverwandtschaften* is no disloyalty to the sphere of *Wilhelm Meisters Wanderjahre oder Die Entsagenden*. It is well known that the former was first conceived as an interlude in the long epic masterpiece, like *The Man of Fifty*, *The Wandering Fair One*, and other such tales and legends. But the poet had deceived himself as to the scope of his theme, he had seen it too small—as it will sometimes happen that a work insists on being bigger than its creator meant it to be. "Such a work," said Goethe later, thanking a discerning friend for finding the book an independent whole, endowed with its own life, "such a work grows under one's hand, it lays on one the duty of dedicating all one's powers to keep it under control and bring it to completion." And so the book which saw the light from Cotta in Tübingen, in 1809, after the sixty-year-old man had spent two years on it and "done his utmost for it," was one of the master's major works, a full-fledged novel in two volumes and two parts : not the greatest of German novels but the noblest.

It is our noblest, and so I have chosen it : an achievement cosmopolitan as it is German, a marvel for its happy and chaste composition, its wealth of association and combination, its unity of effect. For Rochlitz was right when he wrote to Goethe : "However much the digressions, taken singly, would seem to deny it, by so much they affirm it, when looked at as a whole and as parts of a whole." It is a work of such delicate yet relentless understanding of the human heart; it so holds the balance between kindness and severity, candour and reserve, shrewdness and sensibility, feeling and form, that only with astonishment do we call it ours. But since such it is, let me hold it up once more to our own and stranger admiration, as a brilliant example of the heights to which German achievement can rise.

I have clutched in haste at some words of premature eulogy, impatient to be justified of my love without waiting to base it better, impatient too in the name of those who have just read the book for the first time. For what I write is not a preface but an epilogue; intended not to prepare the reader for a feast in store, but to do the friendly office of helping him to collect himself after the reading and to find words for his ensuing emotions. Such, indeed, is the service of love quite essentially laid upon the man of letters; who, when Goethe is his theme, must be peculiarly sensible of the obligation. For what a gift of expression had Goethe himself, what a man of letters he was—if I may thus distinguish between the two talents, of creation and expression! Not but that they may be and are united in the highest type, though Goethe himself employed the antithesis in a way to give us pause, when he referred to himself as "*Schriftsteller*" and to Shakespeare as "*Dichter*." Only to forget it again when sheer love of expression made him boast that he himself was a "*born* writer." And here I feel it in place to praise the *Elective Affinities* as a piece of writing, by quoting the words of the musician Zelter, who on October 27, 1809, wrote to Goethe: "There are certain symphonies of Haydn, whose free, broad movement sets my blood pleasantly flowing and my limbs agreeably tending to outward activity. So it is with me when I read your novels; so it was to-day when I read *Die Wahlverwandtschaften*. That spirited, symbolical playing with the things of this world and the characters you there set up and move about, can never fail of success, whatever else has a place or is made a place for in it. And then the style so well suits—a style composed like that clear element whose nimble denizens flash to and fro, sparkling and darkling, yet never bewildered or lost. One could wax a poet over such a prose—the devil is in it that I cannot so write myself!" The words do the merest justice to the delicacy and dexterity of Goethe's prose, to its vein of pure humanity, to the enchantment of its rhythm. It is a joy to surrender to this last; its magic is rational, being made up of nothing but the finest parts of Eros and Logos.

What I have so far said is enough to indicate that quality in the novel which gives it its human nobility, and of which chiefly I wish to speak: I refer to its exquisite balance. It seems to float poised between the senses and the morals—or, in the realm of æsthetics, between creation and critique, the spontaneous and the calculated. All this not quite without reference to that oft-cited, oft-abused antithesis between the man of letters and the creative artist, which, indeed, is but a phase of the larger antithesis between nature and freedom, commensurate with humanity itself.

But for the moment let us confine ourselves to the field of æsthetics. To begin with, the *Elective Affinities* is, of all Goethe's works, the one which most moves in the realm of the idea. He himself tells Eckermann that it has not in general been his practice as a poet to strive to embody the abstract ; probably the *Wahlverwandtschaften* is the only production of any size in which he consciously laboured to express a comprehensive idea. What he has in mind, of course, is Schiller's immortal essay, *Naive und Sentimentalische Dichtung*, that classic among German essays which comprehends all the others and renders them superfluous—though in its antithetic sphere life and reality are never quite resolved. The field of art has at all times been full of blends of the two, and Schiller's critical discrimination itself errs in theory at one point. In his picture, it is mind only that strives towards nature, towards body ; nature, the naïve, meanwhile resting in herself. But effort is not only in mind, it is also in that towards which mind strives. Nature too is sentimental ; she yearns to be spirit. A high encounter of nature and mind, on their yearning way towards each other—that is man. And a work wherein they meet and mingle may justly be called our noblest and most human. *Elective Affinities* is truly an intellectual production, to an extent not easily found elsewhere in the work of Goethe, the son of nature. The sure touch and the sheer artistry of it were marked down at once by his contemporaries, partly in admiration, but partly too in judgment. A certain meagreness of framework was commented upon, a symmetricality; the briefness of the actual narrative was compared with the long and frequent reflective passages. Solger wrote at the time to Goethe himself that "in the general view the book might almost be called the skeleton of a novel." He praises as "extremely ingenious" the way in which the characters are set off in groups against each other, the members of each group being no little related to each other and yet so widely, so decisively, so consistently distinguished—"yes, in this very variety appear so neatly grouped together." He granted that "at times the characters seem to move more by the will of the author and for the sake of the situation than out of their natures and inner necessities"; yet he stresses too, with satisfaction, his sense that they are not mere "shadowy ideas" but real individuals—though without, he adds, owing much to ordinary personal characteristics. These last "seem more like later retouchings of the picture, meant to make the appearance of reality more deceptive—as deceptive as it is fitting any worthy art should be." Good old Solger! What he considered worthy art has nothing in common with a cinematograph or Madame Tussaud. It is life as thought, characters that, though human beings and not mere "shadowy ideas," are yet transparencies of the idea; and in these words of his he gives us a definition of creative art. The characters in *Elective Affinities* are full of breathing human life. Riemer relates that in Karlsbad society those creatures of the poet's fancy were lived with like flesh and blood, and their likenesses sought among living people. A Charlotte was discovered among the guests of the bath, a Mittler, a Captain, an English Lord. The architect, perhaps best liked of the characters, was at once, on all hands, reported to be a portrait; the original was known, a tall young artist named Engelhardt, from Kassel, must have sat to Goethe for the part. It was even said that the Duchess Louise was the original of Charlotte in this sensational novel; a certain Freiherr von Müffling was the Captain, Fräulein von Reitzenstein the Luciane, and so on. But at the same time the characters are symbols; they are pieces in an exalted game of chess, played in the realm of the idea; they are the embodiments of a nature-mysticism that gives them names like Otto and Ottilie, makes them suffer simultaneous and symmetrical headaches, makes them bring other people's children into the world. I said "at the same time" be it noted, and not "besides." For we are dealing with an interplay of fancy and idea, with flesh-making and spirit-making by turns; with a happy alternation of the "naïve" and the "sentimental," such as would, I imagine, be hard to parallel in the history of art.

And on the moral plane it is the same—save that instead of the words creative and critical, with their implied distinction between the creative artist and the man of letters, we use the other antithesis, of sense and morals, or, speaking historically, of pagan and Christian.

Taken for all in all, Goethe's apparently so confirmed non-Christianity is a very doubtful matter. It is easy—though rather cheap—to quote his humanistic dislike of the "Crucifix"; and better taste, at least, to cite other passages which constitute an explicit expression of reverence for the Christian ideal. In the Pedagogic Province the homage paid to the sanctity of suffering is as significant as it is surprising; and Goethe found in the Gospels the "effective radiance of a sublimity that exhaled from the person of Christ and was of that godlike kind such as only the divine has ever appeared in on this earth." "Higher than the sublime heights of Christianity, higher than its ethical culture as it shines forth from the Gospels," he says with sympathy and a frank sense of fellowship, "the human spirit will hardly reach." He was a follower of Spinoza; and if, indeed, the dualistic separation of God and nature is a fundamental tenet of Christianity, then

Spinoza was a pagan, and Goethe no less. But with God and nature we have not expressed all of the world ; humanity also has place there, and Spinoza's conception of humanity is Christian too, in so far as he defines it as the becoming-conscious of the God-nature in man, as a rending of the web of mere dull being, as liberation from nature and accordingly as spirit. The famous "Mastery of the Passions by Analysis" has absolutely nothing pagan about it; just as little has the Spinozan motif of renunciation (*Entsagung*), which came in time to pervade Goethe's life and work, as freedom did Schiller's and redemption Wagner's.

Of this central motif and its ramifications there would be much to say were there space here. The word *Entsagung* actually appears in the sub-title to *Wilhelm Meister*, of which the *Elective Affinities* is an offshoot. Here I can only state that what Goethe is, in stature and lineaments, in his outline and bulk in the eyes of the nations to-day, is the work of renunciation. This is no general sense. I do not refer to the sacrifice which is the meaning of all art, or to the constructive struggle with chaos, the relinquishment of liberty, the creative self-restraint which is its inner essence. Goethe's pathos—or, since we are dealing not with the ephemeral but with a force which swayed his whole life, his ethos —of renunciation is personal in its nature, it is his destiny. It is the instinctive compulsion of his special and national mission, which was essentially a civilising one. And yet—perhaps the destiny and mission, the obligations and limitations involved in the task of education through renunciation, perhaps after all they are less peculiar to Goethe than they seem ? I submit that they are the precept, the inborn and inviolable imperative of every force in intellectual Germany that will be called in any way or to any degree to shape her destinies—a precept, moreover, that goes unheeded only at the expense of severe mental anguish. I spoke of a sense of Christian fellowship which obviously at moments came over Goethe. What was it, to what had it reference ? Goethe bowed his head before the "ethical culture" of Christianity ; before its humanity, that is, its civilising, anti-barbaric spirit. It was his own. The homage he paid to it on occasion undoubtedly sprang from his insight into this truth ; he assimilated his own mission to that of Christianity within the Germanic world. Here, then, in his conception of his life-task, his national mission, as essentially a civilising one, lies the profoundest, the most Germanic meaning of his "renunciation." Does anybody doubt that there were in Goethe potentialities of a greatness wilder, more exuberant, more perilously "natural" than any to which his instinctive self-control allowed him to give rein, in that highly edifying and representative product as it stands before us to-day ? In his *Iphigenia* the idea of humanity as opposed to barbarism is given the imprint of civilisation—not in the polemical and even political sense in which we use the word to-day, but with the meaning of ethical culture. It was a Frenchman, Maurice Barrès, who called the *Iphigenia* a civilising work, which "defends the rights of society against the arrogance of the intellect." The description fits almost better that other labour of self-discipline and self-chastisement, yes, even of self-mortification, the despised *Tasso*, for whose atmosphere of court and culture and priggishness nobody nowadays has a good word. Both are works of *Entsagen*, of good German self-denial of the advantages of barbarism—that very barbarism in which Richard Wagner so voluptuously revelled, that to-day he reaps, in an ever cruder and cruder popularity, the reward and the just punishment of his ethnical self-indulgence.

But alongside of the *Iphigenia* and the *Tasso* I put the *Elective Affinities*. In language, spirit and conception it represents the height of German civilisation; and wonderful it is to see how society and religion, as contrasted with nature—not hostile to her but merely as "ethical culture"—are here reconciled and united, and how good manners become good morals. The *Elective Affinities* is Goethe's most Christian work; he invoked it to defend himself against the charge of paganism. "I pagan?" he cried. "Did I not let Gretchen be condemned and Ottilie starve to death—isn't that Christian enough for them? What more do they want?" The words betray the pain he felt for those dear children of nature, his creations and sisters, and the sacrifice he made to the moral law in condemning them. One day, six years after he had finished the novel, he was travelling with Sulpice Boisserée from Karlsruhe to Heidelberg, and the stars were coming out. "He began to speak of his relations with Ottilie, how much he loved her, and how unhappy she made him. His language grew strangely resentful." Big, kindly heart, that in all its submission to the decrees of spirit cannot be untrue to nature; that sadly and manfully pays tribute to morality, yet clings to the eternal feminine, and under the starry sky murmurs against the puzzling lot of the humanity which he loves and which makes him unhappy.

"The very simple text of this rambling little book," he wrote, "is the words of Christ: 'Whoso looks upon a woman to desire her,' etc. . . . I do not know if anyone has recognised them in this paraphrase." But that is Tolstoi. Ah, no, it is not Tolstoi; here is no fantasticality of asceticism; not the shattering, involuntary impulse spiritwards of the wild son of nature. It is not, I repeat, anything at all *anti*-nature. We are dealing here with ethical culture, the deepest, most intuitively sympathetic relationship with nature, which is at the same time responsive to the higher command; with a moral conquest by which tragedy is resolved in love and issues in a transfiguration that instructs humanity to view as holy the unresolved tragedy of its own lot.

For Ottilie is holy, is a saint—even though she was not recognised as such when the novel appeared. The book was actually considered shocking. "Every little Wartburg in Germany," as Nietzsche would say, shrieked aloud at the sinfulness of it. As though Christianity the world over has to do with anything but sin, as though sainthood could ever spring from any soil but just that! Ottilie is a saint. Wieland knew it, though he never relished or understood the fact. He too was shocked, from his own point of view, at the "moral purpose" of the work, forsooth! Such was the conflict of opinions. He called it a "truly terrible book"; condemning by the phrase its radical Christianity, which is indeed as absolute as that of the Kreuzer Sonata. Nor could he endure the odour of mortality which clings round it at the close, the "shuddery stillness" to which, Knebel says, "the book mounts towards its end." He fled from it to the lighter, human side, to such delightful scenes as that where Eduard, after his first meeting with Ottilie, says to his wife: "She is a pleasant, entertaining girl," and Charlotte answers, "Entertaining? She never opened her mouth." For this alone, Wieland said, he would, if he were Duke, give Goethe an estate. I quite agree, though I doubt if the liberal old gentleman understood what the pious tale was all about.

The first seed thereof was early planted in Goethe's bosom. As a student he undertook that excursion from Strassburg to Saint Odilienburg in Lower Alsace, which he describes in *Dichtung und Wahrheit*. "Remnants of the old foundation-walls of a Roman stronghold still exist ; and among these ruins and crannies the beautiful daughter of a count is supposed to have withdrawn out of sheer piety and taken up her abode. Travellers edify themselves with a sight of the chapel; they are shown the maiden's spring hard by, and regaled with some charming legends. Her name, and the picture I formed of her, sank deep into my mind. I carried both about with me for long, and at length endowed with them one of my later but not therefore less loved daughters, who was so favourably received by pure and pious hearts." By pure and pious hearts. He is speaking of the book—which after all gave rise to a scandal—as though it were the legend of a saint. The natural science feature was a later addition : I mean the idea, so deeply, strangely and mystically felt, of translating chemical affinities into human terms, of weaving into a love-story the natural and material laws of attraction. All that was so little understood that the Philistines could not see why Goethe "wanted to write two volumes about that chemical business, since he deals only with what is perfectly well known and to be found in a single chapter of any work on chemistry." Could stupidity further go ? Even to-day not everybody appreciates the boldness of clothing the passionate immediacy of man's bond with nature in a symbolism drawn from that science which more than any other has always mingled the mystical and the mathematical. And not only that, but of proceeding to set over against it the conception of man's freedom, and those incalculable powers of the human soul, which can conquer nature, which are above her "laws" and perhaps of a higher order.

Ottilie is the sweetest child of nature ever formed by the hand of art. In her mildness, her smiling speechlessness, her unearthly charm, she has not a little of an Undine, an elemental order of being; her bond with nature is conceived in the very depths of her creator's heart, his love surrounds her like an atmosphere. In her hand the pendulum "strikes" above metal, in the presence of unsuspected coal deposits her left-sided headache comes on. In her sensitive unconsciousness are expressed all the innocence and amorality of nature. She loves by natural law, against the moral. She is Gretchen's sister, like her exposed to sin—yet all that urged her heart unto God was so dear, ah! was so true! Goethe, when he created her, was in love, that is plain. The shadow of Saint Odilie put on sweet flesh and blood from a bodily presence that was near him when he began to write. It was one of his latter flames, kindled in the heart of the fifty-eight-year-old man by the eighteen years of the little *Herzlieb*, foster-daughter to Frommann, the bookseller in Jena. And all the renunciation practised by our confirmed heathen in every single case of his higher "love-life" he here confided to the bosom of this his creature.

From that source emanates the peculiar atmosphere —so hushed, so sweet, so namelessly unearthly— that reigns at the end of the book, when Eduard, Charlotte and Ottilie are living together once more. To the same renunciation is due the awe-inspiring climax, the starvation of Ottilie (cleverly motivated by the reference to her odd lack of appetite when she was at school), the wonder-working powers of her corpse, the strange, seraphic close. The student's dream of the holy Odilie mingles with the resignation of the grey-haired lover to compose a tragic poem which celebrates alike the power of nature and of man, who is above nature and saves himself free through death.

The *Elective Affinities*, in its union of form and thought, is the highest poesy. It is most truly in art what it portrays in idea: the spiritualisation of nature, ethical culture. Always was great art the herald of the third kingdom; art is a pattern for mankind, and the artist, in alliance, as it were, with two powers, art and nature, may well be called the "*Meister*" of mankind.

LESSING

LESSING

(A speech delivered at the Lessing celebration of the Prussian Academy of Art, Berlin)

At times, my friends, the word "classic" has for me a significance which I might almost call mythical; when its accepted meaning—shall we say standard, or exemplary?—seems dry and thin, abstract and bloodless, a diaphanous humanistic conception, to which, even while I accept it, I long to give body and content. For the classic, as I prefer to conceive it, is the prototype in the etymological sense of that word: it is the original, the first living individual embodiment of a form of spirit; the first impression, as it were, of a primitive type, upon which later manifestations, perceiving, will base themselves. A mythus, then, for the type is mythical, and the essence of the myth is recurrence, timelessness, a perpetual present. In this sense only is the classic a prototype, not in the empty sense of exemplar. Classic times, those were patriarchal times, times of the first foundation of the national life.

I say national; for I must attach to the national this conception of a beginning, in order not to embark upon a perfectly shoreless sea, but with some hope of reaching ground firm enough for the mind to pause and rest upon. For whither should we arrive, if we divested the word beginning of all its relative character? There *are* only conditioned beginnings. The world of events is nothing but a stage setting whose shifting scenes lure us from beginnings backward to earlier beginnings and so into the infinite; the beginning of beginnings lying, I suspect, not in time at all, being transcendent. The history of peoples too has many beginnings—as, for example, the history of the German people. But at the beginning of the path we tread to-day, the path of civilisation and action, to follow to whose distant goal is a duty laid upon us, our children and grandchildren, stands the myth, one out of whose calendar of feasts we are celebrating to-day. For first on the route which leads to national unification, for which its intellectual labours broke the ground, laid the foundations, made the path, is our national literature.

The clear-eyed champion whose memory we celebrate to-day was born two hundred years ago in Kamenz, Saxony, and led the life of a free-lance writer. It was Lessing's mission, in virtue of his penetrating understanding, to make divisions and distinctions; yet his genius was unifying. "Before him," so runs a contemporary letter with reference to *Minna von Barnhelm*, "no German author succeeded in inspiring with the same enthusiasm nobility and people, learned and laity alike, or in pleasing them so universally." Goethe praised the "completely north-German national content of the same work, admiring what has since so often been admired, the way in which a specifically north-German product succeeded in delighting the whole of Germany, uniting all Germans in conscious sympathy. While *Nathan der Weise*, our great critic's last word as a poet—uttered in accents of the profoundest wisdom, that evoked from its greatest admirer (Goethe once more) the cry: "May the divine sentiments of patience and tolerance there expressed ever remain precious and sacred in the nation's eyes!" a poetic composition which is the last word in benevolence—*Nathan der Weise* stands for unification of a still higher sort: its conscious pedagogic goal is the peace of mutual understanding, the peace of mankind. This same brave spirit, so national in character and achievement, who as a poet led Germany towards unification, while as dramatic critic he rent asunder the authority of the French canon—he it was who called patriotism a "heroic weakness," and declared that nothing was further from his desire than to be praised as a patriot, a man who would forget that he should be a citizen of the world. The Hamburg dramaturge makes merry over the provincialism of certain comedies of manners, whose author would like to "take the pathetic little traditions of the corner where he was born for the customs of the common fatherland," whereas the truth was that nobody cared a jot "how many times in the year, or where, or when, green cabbage is eaten." Thus he sets against the provincial point of view the intellectual conception of a common fatherland—the national, this is, against, or at least above, the sectional. But he is also aware of a point of view wherein the national in its turn appears as the sectional; he expresses it in the wish that "there might be in every state men who are above popular prejudice and know precisely when patriotism ceases to be a virtue." Those are his words—the words of a free man and a genuine. They imply that the intellectual and the humane are only a heightening and extension of the natural and national, and they make plain that the trend to further unification lies inherent in the national idea itself, though all unrecognised by those tribal-minded exclusionists who, in amazing miscomprehension inscribe the latter on their banner and see in it nothing but the slogan of segregation and animosity.

Lessing's national mission was one of clarification by criticism. His was a penetrating and inspired understanding. Nathan's phrase, "we must distinguish," might be set as a motto above his great analytical contributions, the *Laocoön*, the *Hamburger Dramaturgie* and the theological controversies. Definition, limitation, lucid statement were his peculiar joy and gift; they were, to employ once more that singularly pregnant word, his mission. For singularly pregnant it is, that in the conception, with its implication of task, function and tool, there is an interplay of the personal and the supra-personal imperative. When a young nation girds itself up to a heightening and burgeoning of its culture, certain duties lie upon it: to put its intellectual house in order, to stabilise theory and law, to lay down national principles, to distinguish and clarify. And these become gift and mission, passion and mastery, in a man who may, at moments, think of himself as a teacher, but with all his shrewdness certainly never draws a line between the impulse that urges him on and the tasks that grow to him out of the depth of the general.

Lessing was from the first the founder of a mythical type—mythical because it constantly reappears in the flesh. He is the classical creative intelligence, the patriarch of the writing tribe. Most personally and vividly he represents the ideal productive type, the kind of intellectual whose performance is viewed in some quarters with a jaundiced eye, as mere profane writing, sharply and contemptuously distinguished from the sacred sphere of the afflatus. We all know how popular this distinction is, particularly in Germany, and particularly now. Our current critique simply lives on it. And at bottom, I feel, it partakes of that same stuffiness, that provincial, "green-cabbage" point of view of which Lessing spoke. It is self-righteous and spiteful; nor is its position tenable, since the line between creative authorship and mere "writing" runs, of course, not outwardly, between the products, but inwardly, within the personality itself; and because it is possible to imagine, combined in one person, the trained writer endowed with initiative and the conscious, clear-eyed creative artist who could say:

> "*Ich bin nicht kalt. Ich sehe wahrlich*
> *Nicht minder gern, was ich in Ruhe sehe.*"

Lessing's own classic personality is a proof that the combination exists. The enthusiasts of simplification underestimate the awkwardness of a distinction which is constantly being blurred and obliterated through the critical factor of language itself. An art whose medium is language will always show a high degree of critical creativeness, for speech is itself a critique of life: it names, it characterises, it passes judgment, in that it creates. There is, of course, such a thing as detachment, objectivity—the "sacred sobriety" of which a certain hymnist speaks. But it must have followed the intoxication, on that being felt as something which needed checking. Detachment, indeed, is not productive, but it is possible to conceive of creation and craftsmanship as different stages in the development of a work, united by an act of cool objectivation. We need waste no praise on this last—but then, neither need we deny it relationship with the will to morality. Again, the enthusiasts of simplification forget, or do not observe, how the conscious and the unconscious dovetail into each other in the productive; or how much of the naïve, the unconscious—of the dæmonic, to use their own sinister word—enters into and determines all conscious action.

The type which we are analysing possesses a self-critical acumen, a modesty and candour which unfortunately play all too easily into the hands of those who would deny its claims to membership in the charmed circle of creative artists. Such a man typically runs to meet adverse criticism, not to forestall it, but because he has an objective eye on his own performance. He it is who always says the best things about himself—not complimentary things, but conveying the truth as he sees it, however black and forbidding. Then the others parrot it after him, seldom to his credit, and rather to be able to use his own words against him : "He said so himself, you know." Lessing's love of truth is essentially radical ; he has an ungovernable gift for "hunting out the truth in the very last hole," as he puts it ; there would of course be a peculiar zest in the game when self-knowledge was the prize. Some pleasing instances of the thing I mean are to be found in his own creative work ; as when Minna says to Tellheim that there is a certain hard, casual way of referring to one's own misfortunes, and Tellheim hastens to answer, "Which at bottom is only boasting and complaining too." Or in *Emilia Galotti*, when Conti the painter speaks of his dissatisfaction with himself as an artist, adding : "And yet I am sometimes quite satisfied with my own lack of self-satisfaction."

Lessing, paying homage to the critical spirit, and disowning the complaint that it acts as a wet-blanket to genius, asserts that to it alone he owes all that is tolerable in his work, and that he flatters himself to have won from it something akin to genius. "I am neither actor nor poet," he says. "I do not feel in myself the living spring that rises by its own power and shoots upward in such streams of richness, freshness and purity. With me everything must come out through pressure and pipes." How they have been quoted against him, the pressure and pipes! But if he was right, not so were the others who quoted him. In Lessing's world, truth is very relative—one gets used to that. It becomes humanised, as it were, the criteria lying less in the matter under dispute than in its defender. Goethe never concurred in these judgments of Lessing about himself. The influence he wielded, Goethe says, in the long run gave the lie to his detractors. Goethe was all for letting the end try the man. But if one cannot wait for the judgment of time, then surely one may cite the pre-eminent qualities of personality, originality, boldness. Genius, one may say, betrays itself in the unexpected, in the sudden coming-to-be of something undreamed-of beforehand. It manifests itself in the possibility of something new of its kind, which could be triumphantly valid only by the power of personality. Genius in art, then, would be the surprise, the wonder and enchantment, the something dared that seemed quite impossible until it was done. In the light of this definition the old question as to Lessing's rank as an author becomes demonstrably idle. For creations like Minna and Nathan bear precisely this imprint of the new and the surprising, of something risked that became possible only by dint of being done, valid and triumphant only by virtue of the mingled characteristics of shrewdness and naïveté. They may, because they can—and only so. Less vital than they are they could not maintain themselves. And in face of this objective artistry, this disarming intelligence, this cordial good sense rising to the highest pitch of amenity, it would be callous and pedantic to challenge its claim to the title of creative art.

Such was Otto Ludwig's view: he said of *Minna von Barnhelm* that the old indictment must fall, in view of an art that could so swell out a single seed-corn of matter as to make of it a play of inexhaustible interest. And yet it is just this art of "swelling out," of irresistibly, inexplicably enlarging upon, which constitutes another trait of the classic type which I describe. Invention is not its strong point; but it can invest the detail, and the uttermost detail, with rich and unfailing charm. It has small concern with plot, and lacking talent therein dispenses with all but the minimum required to give backbone to the composition. Its strength lies in the power to give that little effectiveness and beauty: digging it in, building it out, exploiting it, sharpening its lines, accenting its facets, illuminating the obscurest corner of its theme, until what would in another's hand be boresome becomes genuinely entertaining. All this, I repeat, is no less characteristic of the type than is its self-critical candour. But in the first place, there is something Dürerish, something of the German *Meister* about this careful, busy, ingenious activity, this lively reverence for detail, which cannot be condemned as lacking all communion with the muses. And in the second place, this bareness out of which a virtue grows may be conceived as the truest badge of creative authorship—at least Schopenhauer says that the greatest works succeed with the minimum of contrivance.

The case is the same with the third trait of the type, the characteristic which we might call its masculinity, or its preoccupation with the masculine. The male suits incomparably better than the female its talent for characterisation. Its men are drawn with more depth, power, certainty. Minna is admittedly far outranked by the melancholy and meticulous Tellheim. To begin with, he is much more masculine than she is feminine—a fact for which old Mendelssohn accounted by saying that Lessing was most successful with those characters which were nearest his own—as, for instance, with Tellheim, Odoardo and the Templar. The last has always been considered the freshest and most vivid characterisation of youth upon the German stage, or any stage. It was Friedrich Schlegel who remarked upon how thoroughly Lessing's characters are Lessingised.

It is a mark of the type—we might well call it lyrical subjectivity, and thus derive it from the explicitly and peculiarly poetic !

Again, there is a certain proud economy of output, the opposite to unintelligent productivity. Lessing presents a comedy—*the* comedy : as if to say, "See, this is the way to do it !" His pride, and his critical dignity forbid him to follow it with ten poorer ones ; he passes on to another form. Such shrewdness, such self-awareness are surely to be appraised higher than dull, haphazard, uneven performance—surely they rank as artistic gift, and if so, then poetic.

But poetic the medium of our type is not. His language is not poetic. Not in the Orphic sense, not high, not a mystery. There is much justice in the accusation that it is dry, that it wants feeling and acme. It does not mount as high as the sources, the fount and spring of our idiom. It is simply cultured, pithy and shrewd. It demands of itself merely clarity, neatness, precision : "*d'être clair et précis*," as Lessing himself puts it. That it does not lack vigour is rather remarkable. On the contrary, it aims at and attains that quality in considerable degree, for it has the gift of appositeness, and of a phrasing that makes it at once discursive and dramatic. If our type set itself one day to compose verse, it will be prosaic, like Nathan's, spoken, not sung ; very pleasant to hear, not lacking in rhythm, but without *melos*, having no meltingness ; such uninspired verse, indeed, that Friedrich Schlegel could speak of its "disillusioned note." And yet verse of such golden-hearted good sense that unless you have steeled your heart beforehand you yield to it none the less. Marvellous, the power wielded by such dry good sense! Goethe was "quite bowled over" (*ordentlich prosterniert*). He is said never to have tired of praising *Nathan* as the loftiest masterpiece of human skill. To quote Schlegel once more, Lessing was "the Prometheus of German art." In the beautiful funeral oration pronounced by Herder over his grave, Lessing's prose was declared to be the most original since Luther. Truly, if this German was not poetic it was so much else that it can afford to renounce the vague title to honour which the adjective conveys.

We might go on to cite other weak points in Lessing's armour; they would be just so many traits of the type of which he is the classic example. His sensuous equipment was slight, his demands in this respect amounting almost to indifference—for instance, in the *Laocoön*, in his treatment of antique sculpture, his senses never absolve him from the duty of analysis. And yet this in many ways superannuated investigation into the line of demarcation between painting and poetry contains here and there an *aperçu* that is certainly creatively felt. Take that painful perception of the law that language can only praise, not reproduce beauty; that challenge to the poet to give up description and instead paint for us the satisfaction, the sympathy, the love, the delight that beauty confers—"for thereby," says he, "you have painted beauty herself." Possible that this anti-descriptive flight into the lyrical constitutes Lessing's approach to the dramatic. Otherwise, there lies no little irony in the fact that this prosaic, half-acknowledged poet, with his limited powers of imagination, should have chosen as a medium of self-expression precisely that creative art-form which since Aristotle has passed for the highest in every school of æsthetics. And not only chosen it, but vivified it in a way that may fairly be called epoch-making.

Or was it the quality of logic in the drama that attracted Lessing, was it the dialectician in him that made him a dramatist ? Here we come upon another and most striking trait of our mythical type—the one which above all others makes the man of temperament misdoubt its right to poetic rank. The tendency to polemic—what he himself called the spitfire irascibility (*Spitzbübin Irascibilität*), the love of controversy for its own sake—runs through all his works. He puts in the pepper and salt, sometimes slyly, sometimes with reckless hand ; the passion for seasoning grows upon him apace, until it seems that he finds the merely creative and dramatic very flat by contrast. Now the view that the poet must not be a controversialist is deep-rooted in the German mind. He is supposed to accept all phenomena as they come, with calm and lofty simplicity, and then transmute them. He is degraded and dishonoured if he display any feeling about the times or the world he lives in, any sensitiveness towards its bad, or base, or stupid manifestations. He is descending into the market-place, he is "mixing in trade." World and reality are obviously so well aware of their own innate commonness as perforce to despise whoever makes himself common with them. The right sort of poet, they feel, is a creature who sees nothing, marks nothing, suspects nothing, and whose "pure" foolishness is as wax in the hands of baser interests. If he does see anything, if he runs the gauntlet against shams and injustices and the besotting of the people, against the lying confusion between, shall we say, high-flown patriotism and big business, then he is no poet but a "writer," and an unpatriotic one to boot.

So that if anything could bring Lessing's good name as a poet into disrepute with his countrymen it would be his zeal in polemic. Heine has put it most wittily: Lessing, the giant, he says, in his rage let fly a few random rocks at certain nonentities —to whom then these rocks served as grave-stones to keep them from being forgotten. Lessing himself was not insensible to the superfluity of honour which he showed to some of his opponents. "I should not like," he wrote of one of his controversies, "to have the value of this enquiry measured by its occasion. That is so despicable that only the way in which I have used it can excuse me for wanting to use it at all." To which he appends a little apologia for polemic which even to-day is entirely pertinent. "Not, indeed," he says, "that I did not regard our modern public as a bit too squeamish with regard to controversy or anything suggesting controversy. It seems to want to forget that it owes to sheer contradiction its enlightenment on many subjects of first importance, and that if human beings had never yet quarrelled over anything in this world neither would they be of one mind over anything to this day."

Scepticism, denial, the tendency to these, not merely form a trait of the classic type which Lessing founded; doubt is its native heath, its religion, the soil in which it lives and flourishes. Doubt as belief, scepticism as a positive passion—such is quite genuinely the paradox exhibited by Lessing. It is a paradox of the heart and not of the understanding; and one with it is a conception of truth which scarcely occurs in such flower a second time in the history of the human intellect. We have already seen how Lessing makes truth relative to the human element. Man, he asserts, proves his worth not in the possession or the supposed possession of truth, but in the sheer pains he has taken to come at it. That is to subjectivate the value of truth and almost truth itself. It implies a profound philosophic doubt of the objective, together with a passion for research, as which alone he envisages human morality. For how false it would be to confuse this philosophic doubt with nihilism, with intentional malice! He once said of his *Nathan der Weise*: "It is not at all a satirical piece, such as ends with a burst of mocking laughter. It is an affecting piece, such as I have always written." Instead of satirical he would have said nihilistic, had the word been current in his time. His scepticism is as far from flippancy as is his wit, which is a scorching wit, but not supercilious—a genuine expression of his way of reacting to life. He is witty even in the letter where he describes the birth and death of his little Traugott, written while his wife lay dying. Wittiest of all he is when some display of sanctimonious orthodoxy rouses his wrath and dips his restless pen in gall. He it was who spoke the immortal words: "If God held all the truth in his closed right hand and in his left the single ever-living urge towards truth, though with the proviso that I must forever err, and said to me 'Choose!' I should bow down humbly before his left hand and say, 'Father, give me this. Pure truth is for thee alone!'" Note the fervour of the utterance. These are not the accents of irreligion, but of a religious doubt that approaches a worship of the infinite and a perpetual striving towards it.

But what orthodoxy saw therein was a stiff-necked rejection of revelation. This great Protestant had angered literal Lutheranism to the core; it sought—but in vain—to provoke him in the struggle to a compromising admission of his actual beliefs. It looked as though Lessing fought, not so much in behalf of some truth, or of truth in general, as out of a passion for administering small dagger-thrusts that should rouse his opponents out of their comfortable intellectual and spiritual landlordism. And yet the theological controversy with Hauptpastor Goeze is very far from being a satirical or nihilistic performance. There is no "burst of mocking laughter" about it ; it is "touching and kindly, such as I have always written." In its fine-tempered ductability, its calm in the face of provocation, in the brilliance of its sallies, in its high seriousness, it is very probably his best work; I would even say his best creative work. It is easier to see this to-day, now that its theology has ceased to be anything but background and *point d'appui* for ethical and intellectual generalisations.

"The letter is not the spirit"—this is Lessing's position and his theme. It is a position that out-Luthers Luther, carrying him on beyond the text and the letter ; by it he probably meant to suggest the saving of religion and the spirit, since the letter was no longer to be saved. For was it not short-sighted of Luther to base religion on the Bible alone, since that must one day fall a sacrifice to the critics ? But this discrimination between the spirit and the letter would mean the saving of the Bible too from the crude enthusiasm of those who would have it that the spirit is naught without the letter. True, in Lessing's glorious controversial writings there comes into play so much irony, so much veiled allusion, so much dialectical virtuosity, so much tactical dissembling, that after all some confusion is inevitable. Even the virtuosity is confusing, as being the product not of callousness, vanity or satiric bent, but of a deep seriousness, passionate and "touching." Was Lessing really seeking to save Christianity, by saying that it had been there before the Scripture and would be when the Scripture was no more ? Yet he wrote a twelfth "Anti-Goeze," the *Nathan* ; and of it he said that he would be content if it taught one out of a thousand readers to doubt the evidence and the universality of his religion. And if this religion were Christianity—what then ? Lessing was more radical than he dared to express ; but it was precisely in his ambiguity that he was radical. In order to be a thorn in the side of bigoted Lutheranism he chimed in with the Catholics ; on the other hand, he was offensive to rationalists and the enlightenment, and had more sympathy with downright orthodoxy than with the half-way kind watered down with liberalism. Was that perfidy and bad faith ? The nation in general never found it so ; Lessing has always been considered a pattern of courage and manliness. Only this manliness, this trustworthiness was not of a simple kind, but such as an artist can possess, varied and played upon by his art, not only in the matter of form but likewise in that ultimate passion which is the organic secret of all creation. Precisely when Lessing seemed to stand right, he was standing farther left than anything his age could conceive.

And so when this greatest Protestant between

Luther and Nietzsche takes the field against a literal interpretation of the Scriptures and the proselytising romanticism of the Catholic Church seizes on his sallies and turns them to the advantage of the Roman tradition and authority, it is hard to conceive anything more disingenuous. But at least the fact is evidence—the only piece of its kind in Germany—that brains can fight on the side of reaction. Even so, Catholic romanticism should have too much pride to wish to yoke to her chariot a spirit so diametrically opposed to hers. But how much worse still is the only too common sight, that of plain and simple un- and anti-intelligence counterfeiting and dressing itself out in the gifts of the spirit ! How many times to-day has the new truth had occasion to cry out to those who think that everything is grist to their mill : "That was not what we meant !"

No, it was not meant as Clemens Brentano would have it mean. For it was the spirit of Luther and no other that Lessing invoked against Lutheranism. "Great, misunderstood man ! Thou hast freed us from the yoke of tradition ; but who is to free us from the intolerable yoke of the letter ? Who will give us at last a Christianity *such as thou wouldst teach it now*, as Christ himself would teach it ?" "*Wie Du es itzt lehren würdest !*" That is perfect Lessing. It is the formula for all the spiritual, living present, that the letter, that history, would slay. And misunderstood is every great genius whom the yesterday-men will not see as *historically* great, conditioned and limited by the century that bore him ; taking him literally instead, invoking his authority precisely against that which he, or his like, would teach now. Their error is great, when they yearn for the great man of yesterday back again, thinking he would be on their side. If he came, they would not know him. A French writer has finely said that a masterpiece must not look like a masterpiece. There may be exceptions : the masterpiece of the day may appear in the half-burlesque mask of the historic, uniting the appeal of the familiar and prized with that of the new and daring, when your genuine conservative will scent the parody and brand it as profane. But though this may happen now and again, yet the French writer's dictum applies not only in the realm of art but for all life, all being and becoming in time. A man in whom the conservatives, the people with their heads fixed on backwards, think to recognise a reincarnation of a past genius, is in all probability not the great man of to-day. That full-blooded, mighty and pugnacious man, Hauptpastor Goeze, as he stood with his fist on the Bible and his rockfast faith in the revealed Word, must have looked to the short-sighted far more like the historic Luther than did the volatile Lessing, dissembler and sceptic, and altogether less Lutheran than Fritzian to the view. But Pastor Goeze was not the "new Luther," merely a Luther stuck fast in the toils of time ; whereas the really new, the modern Luther, was Lessing.

He himself, once so living and present, is now an historical figure ; his one-sided—and once so salutary—tendency to rationalism, his doctrine of an abstract virtue, put into the mouth of Nathan, that all too humanly sweeps away the conception of *religio* and will hear nothing of any inborn and positive faith-content, is to-day no longer quite viable. The enlightenment whose true son and faithful knight Lessing always, despite all temperamental irregularities, remained, is to-day intellectually out of date ; it has made way for a fuller-blooded, deeper, more tragic conception of life. All this is undeniable. Yet the modern Lessing would still, I think, be minded to enter the field against the further swing of the pendulum. We are so far gone in the irrational—to the joy of all baser enemies of light, all priests of the dynamistic orgasm—that it now looks like an evil and dangerous rebound, and a rebound against the rebound will by degrees become inevitable. The chthonic crew has already had too much water to its mill ; it must be frightened back into the darkness whither it belongs by mother-right. The spirit of the historic Lessing has a task to-day ; its importance must not be under-estimated, despite all modern, anti-rational hostility to mind, all that anti-idealism which forms one side—but only one—of Nietzsche's mind-drunken prophecy, and which, in both morals and politics, is highly susceptible of abuse. In Lessing's name and spirit let it be ours to aim beyond every type of fascism at a union of blood and reason, which alone merits the name of complete humanity.

This great controversialist of ours did not become nihilistic, did not "leave the field with a burst of mocking laughter." He was kindly. And this his nation, and all the nations, should count it his highest claim to praise. He pondered long and deeply. That he then made play with the conclusions to which he came was not done for the sake of the play. His was a spirit as full of faith, love and hope as any that has lived and taken thought for the lot of man. He, manliest of spirits, had faith in the coming of an age of humanity. Let me end on those words in which he bore witness to his faith, words full of an inward emotion that lifts his usual lively clarity of style to a level but seldom—and then how movingly—attained by him: "Wise Providence, move onward, at thine own unnoted pace. But let me never, because I mark not, despair of thee, even when thy step seems to tend backwards. It is not true, that the shortest line is always the straight one."

NIETZSCHE AND MUSIC

NIETZSCHE AND MUSIC

Far be it from me, ladies and gentlemen, to detain you for long, with my modest words, from enjoyment of that nobler language which music speaks. It is not, God be praised, my office to hold anything like a critical or literary discourse on Nietzsche. The task assigned me has regard for the fact that my powers would fail, that I should be tongue-tied with embarrassment and modesty at the idea of delivering a speech in public, attempting formal mastery over a theme which was of such basic importance to me personally in the shaping of my own mind, and has left so indelible an imprint upon it. No, all that I have been asked to do is to tell you in a few words the purpose of our meeting and the reason why it has taken this form.

But even to explain why we have chosen to celebrate not in words but with music the memory of that ruling spirit, strong in prophecy and in enlightenment, in whose name we are assembled, is to avow at once what he means to us to-day—in what sense, at this particular moment for us and for Europe, we acknowledge him as our master.

He loved music as no one else has loved it—so much in justification of our choice. He was a musician. No other art was so near his heart as this ; every other made way for it in his consciousness, in his sympathies. He distinguished between eye-men and ear-men, and counted himself among the latter. Of the plastic arts he has said little or nothing, and they obviously had for him but small significance. Language and music—these were the sphere of his experiences, his productivity, his affairs of the heart and the mind. His language itself is music ; with a refinement of ear, a masterly sense of cadence and *tempo*, a prose rhythm that before him were unexampled in German and probably in European literature. And it is not only the relationship and inner accord between criticism and poetry which is displayed by the phenomenon we know as Nietzsche—this phenomenon of the poet in the realm of knowledge. We perceive at the same time the peculiar affinity, the inner unity, between criticism and music, continuously and creatively functioning in the personality of this genius. Now it is in the nature of criticism to classify and distinguish ; and it was in the realm of music that the noblest critical functionings of Nietzsche's mind and soul, of his commandingly prophetic spirit, found play.

In a word, his relation to music was one of passion. But passion—the word, of course, derives from suffering ; and what part, and wherefore, does an element of suffering play in the conception ? What is it makes lovers suffer? It is doubt. Nietzsche once said that the love of a philosopher for life is like the love of a man for a woman he does not trust. The same, precisely, might have been said of his love for music. It was love that bore a thorn of doubt, hence it was passion; and if ever passion has been defined as doubting love, the definition bore Nietzsche's sign-manual.

The question is, whence came those prophetically edifying scruples of conscience and doubts of authority which gave his love of music its sting? If I may guess, they arose because he—in this a very German—placed music on the same level with the romantic, and it was his lot, his mission and his heroic destiny, to put himself to the touch upon that so seductive master-complex of the soul, the musical-romantic and romantic-musical—and thus almost the German—complex.

His heroism, however, consisted in self-conquest. In behalf of life, he fought the "ascetic ideal" with all the strength of his genius; but he himself was a hero of that *ascesis* of the inner world which is the ethical side of revolution. Like Wagner, from whom he parted on grounds of his conscience but whom he loved unto death, he was by origin a later son of the romantic movement. But Wagner was a self-realising, self-glorifying child of fortune, Nietzsche a revolutionary with self-conquest as his goal; thus it fell out that while Wagner was the end of an epoch—however fully, however gloriously, with whatever compelling enchantment—Nietzsche has become seer and guide into a new future for humanity.

This he is to us : a friend of life, a seer of our higher humanity, a leader into new worlds, a teacher who teaches us to conquer everything in ourselves which stands opposed to life and to the future—in other words, to romanticism. For the romantic is a song of nostalgia for the past—it is the beguiling song of death ; and the phenomenon of Richard Wagner, which Nietzsche so dearly loved and which his ruling spirit drove him to exorcise, was no other than the paradoxical and eternally interesting phenomenon of world-conquering obsession with death.

I well know how much in you—in all of us, despite Nietzsche, despite Goethe himself—rises up against the thought of the romantic as morbid and antagonistic to life. For is not the romantic the sweetest and wholesomest thing in the world, goodness itself, born as it is in the deepest depth of the folk-soul ? Yes, no doubt. But it is a fruit, splendidly fresh and sound for its moment, and yet extraordinately prone to decay ; the purest refreshment to the spirit if enjoyed at the right moment, yet at the next, the wrong moment, spreading rottenness and corruption among men. It is a fruit of life, conceived of death, pregnant of dissolution ; a wonder of the soul, perhaps the highest, in the eye, and sealed with the blessing of conscienceless beauty, but on cogent grounds regarded with mistrust by the eye of a responsible and controlling love of life, and a subject for self-conquest at the definite behest of conscience.

Yes, self-conquest—that might well be the essence of triumph over this love, this soul-enchantment with the sinister consequences! We are all its sons and know its power. Some soul-enchanting artist might give to this nostalgic song a giant volume and with it subdue the world. Kingdoms might be founded on it, earthly, all too earthly kingdoms, solid, progressive, not at all nostalgic, in which the song would degenerate, if I may say so, into a piece of gramophone music. But its truest son may still have been he who consumed his life in self-conquest and died; on his lips the new word of love which as yet he scarce knew how to speak, that we can scarcely stammer, the prophetic word of love for life and the future.

But self-conquest looks sometimes not unlike self-betrayal and even like betrayal in general. And Nietzsche's great, his representative act of self-conquest, the so-called apostasy from Wagner, looked like that. His friends complained that no good could come to a man who was always sawing off the branch he sat on; and the best book on Nietzsche, by Ernst Bertram, has a chapter called "Judas." But it is because Nietzsche became a Judas that to-day all believers in the future invoke his name—and not the name of that imperial romanticist—and that he has become the evangelist of a new alliance of earth and man.

The highest, the most critical decisions his conscience had to make, were bound up, as I said, with music. Music tried his heroic mould, through it he found resolution and redemption. "Music and tears," he once wrote, "I scarcely know them apart." We do well, then, to keep his memory with music; with the noblest music, performed by the most gifted master of the instrument upon which, we are told, he was an extempore master. I am happy to give over, to listen with you, and to think that he listens with us.

DÜRER

DÜRER

THE thought of Dürer always calls up in my mind another name, Nietzsche's—to invoke whose pure and holy spirit, wherein are united so much of our heroic past and so much of our future, means to summon at once the profoundest memories and the highest hopes. Nietzsche was the medium through which I learned to know Dürer's world. Through him I looked, I divined, I grasped through my emotions—as is youth's fashion, since, by nature indifferent to history, it is scarcely aware of the past save through the present, which does not, indeed, instruct in it, yet speaks for it by letting it shine through. Does Nietzsche mention Dürer? I could not tell. But what has he in mind, when he speaks of Schopenhauer and his authority, which first encouraged Wagner's feminine art in the direction of the ascetic ideal? He says: "What does it signify, when a genuine philosopher pays homage to the ascetic ideal, a self-poised mind, like Schopenhauer, a man and a gallant knight, stern-eyed, with the courage of his own strength, who knows how to stand alone and not wait on the nod and beck of superior officers?" What has he in mind—or, if he has not, what does he mean by this peculiarly precise and explicit description of moral straightforwardness and manliness? Would one be wrong to write the name of Dürer in the margin at this place? And one might well add certain lines by Goethe, written in momentary forgetfulness of his classicistic irritation at "*trübe Form und bodenlose Phantasie*" and characterising the essence of Dürer's nature:

> "*Ihr festes Leben und Männlichkeit,*
> *Ihre innere Kraft und Ständigkeit.*"

Dürer, Goethe, Schopenhauer, Nietzsche, Wagner—there it would all be, in one quotation with two glosses: the whole fateful complex and galaxy, a whole world, the German world, with all its vaulting self-dramatisation, its enthralling intellectualistic climax and dissolution at the end—and yet not at the end. For beside the great wizard and conjurer stands the seer and conqueror: the myth itself alongside the theatrical exploiter of the myth, the hero and the sacrifice, the herald of the new and higher humanity.

My youth, I may remark, did not prevent me from recognising the moralist in Nietzsche—at a time when he meant little to the public save a childish misinterpretation of the superman idea. But the preconditions, the intellectual origins of the moral tragedy which was his life—that immortal European drama of self-discipline, self-conquest, self-crucifixion, with mental death as its heart-breaking, mind-staggering close—they lie, they are to be found nowhere else than in the protestantism of the Nuremberg pastor's son, in that Nordic, German, middle-class moral sphere, Dürer's sphere, the scene of "The young knight, Death and the Devil," which in all his wanderings remained the home of Nietzsche's soul. "I like in Wagner," he wrote to Rohde in October 1866, "what I like in Schopenhauer : the moral fervour, the Faustian flavour, the Cross, Death and the Tomb." It was at this time that he went three times in one Passion Week in Basle to hear the Matthew Passion. "The Cross, Death and the Tomb." Here we have another essential element of the German and Dürer character-world, intimately bound up with the "Männlichkeit und Ständigkeit," the knightliness between the Devil and Death ; passion, odour of the tomb, sympathy with suffering, Faustian *melencolia*—and all of it composed into an idyll of peaceful, industrious domesticity, with the sun shining warm on the death's head through the bottle-glass in the window-panes, and hour-glass and lion lending dignity and a glimpse of the eternal to the modest, humble little scene.

But what else has it ? What else, besides love, and memories, and a pattern, has this world of which we speak bequeathed to us through its succession of masters : what else decisive for our characters and destinies, entering into the very inmost nature of us all ? For one thing, the graphic art of Germany ;

since the love of the German artist, whether in literature or art, is given not to colour but to line. And then, much else besides, much that is splendid, much that is shamefaced ; much matter for pride, much that is hard to confess—and both well known to everybody. For here our conception of the master-craftsman, noblest of all our national treasures in the idea, our highest, most revered, most unifying, has its origin. What rank in the world, what power and honour and acclaim, could surpass in the German mind the simple and intrinsically lofty conception of the *Meister* ? Where else more easily could varying counsels still find themselves at one to-day, than in the ideal of the master-craftsman, with its uprightness, sincerity, love of the task ; its mellowness of life and art, its moral and intellectual leadership ? In the conception respectability is united with a dash of that daring which Goethe ascribes to every artist. From industry comes depth of vision, and greatness is born out of care for the small. Patience and heroism, the dignified and the doubtful, love of the past and claims upon the unknown—all this united to make one whole. Ah, and how much else —how much of our remote and primitive heritage, of our profoundly national insufficiency, our angular uncouthness has a part in this world of German art, this day-dreaming world where child and greybeard meet : perversely scrupulous, dæmonic and ribald at once, sick with infinity, shamefacedly yet honourably laying bare its pedantry, its philistinism, its self-torment, its anxious calculation, its laborious introspection—all this flowing together with that consummateness, that stout persistence, that obstinate yearning displayed by a valour that will not give way to self, that goes to meet the remotest difficulty, that spoils a piece of work and makes it useless rather than put it down before wreaking the uttermost upon it.

To think of Dürer means to love, to smile, to remember. It means to be aware of the profoundest, the most super-personal, of all that lies outside of and below the corporeal limits of our ego, but yet nourishes and conditions it. It means history as myth, history that is ever fresh and ever present. For we are much less individuals than we either hope or fear to be.

TOLSTOI

TOLSTOI

(On the hundredth anniversary of his birth)

HE had the proportions of the nineteenth century, this giant: he bore up under epic burdens which would have crushed our own puny and short-winded generation. And how great was the epoch to which Tolstoi belonged—in all its gloom, its materialism, its moral austerity, its scientific brusquerie! How great the generation of creative geniuses who dominated the five decades before 1900! Is our own time, whatever advantage it may show or begin to show over that vanished epoch—our modicum of enlightenment, of intellectual progress, our glimpse, still faint, into possibilities of a blither and prouder sense of humanity—is it really entitled to its superior and scornful attitude toward its predecessor? Especially since it would be hard to deny that morally speaking it has fallen far behind? Much, very much of the misprision and violence done to the idea and to human dignity, which our age complacently pockets up—for which it will stand in history—would not have been borne by the "fatalistic" nineteenth century. Often, in 1914, it occurred to me that the war would not have dared to break out if the keen, shrewd eyes of that old man at Yasnaya Polyana had still been open on the world. A childish idea, no doubt. Anyhow, history would not have it so. He was not there, nor anybody like him. The reins of Europe slipped, she had no master—nor has she to-day.

Tolstoi said of his early work, *Childhood and Youth*: "Modesty aside, it is something like the Iliad." That was simple truth, and—on extrinsic grounds only—the comment fits even better the gigantic achievement of his maturity, *War and Peace*. The Homeric, the timeless epic vein was strong in Tolstoi, as perhaps in no other artist in the world. His work has the epic's long oceanic swell, its majestic monotone; its powerful, astringent freshness and tang, its immortal healthiness and realism. For the two conceptions—health and realism—are allied, mentally we see and feel them as one; we may attempt—as I have elsewhere done more at length—to delimit this naïve and plastic world of noble and natural childlikeness, by contrasting it with the world of disease and the nobility born of spirit—in other words, with Schiller's idealistic and Dostoiewsky's apocalyptic world of shadows. There was a time when surprise and wonder greeted the conjunction of the two names, Goethe and Tolstoi, but recent criticism has accepted the parallel and found it psychologically illuminating. It would be pedantic and arbitrary to try to apply it farther than in fundamentals. Useless to insist on the differences in mental atmosphere, geographical and historical factors—they are too obvious. So soon as we apply a cultural test: the formula of nature striving toward spirit and the corresponding urge of spirit towards nature—we have destroyed the conception of a relationship which up to then had been so charmingly and mystically intimate. For we must in honour admit that, possessing Goethe, we can but find the struggles of Tolstoi, that son of nature, toward spirit, tragically foundering as they did in the fantastic and the absurd, to be the noble but helpless wrestling of a childlike barbarian toward the true and the human—a spectacle at once great and pathetic.

And yet, artistically considered, it is just this titanic helplessness of his that lends Tolstoi's works their enormous moral weight. His narrative power is incomparable; to come into contact with it—even at a time when he scorned and despised his art and only employed it by habit, as a means of propagating his doubtful and depressing moral creed—brings to him with talent to receive it (no one else can) streams of refreshment, power, primeval health and a lust of creation. It is not a question of imitation—how could power like that be imitative? A pupil of Tolstoi who deserved the name would hardly be recognisable as such; under that master-influence he might practise his art in many a way, various in both form and spirit, and above all in a way different from his master's. Tolstoi himself, an Antaeus, at each repeated contact with his mother-earth went sublimely from strength to strength; and now his great self-constituted creative work has in turn become to us earth and nature, itself a phenomenon. To read him, to be played upon by his animal keenness of observation, the sheer *élan* of his creative onslaught, the perfectly transparent rationality of his plastic artistry, as unclouded as Goethe's own by any trace of mysticism, is to escape from all danger of sickly and superficial trifling by a return to the healthy and the primeval, to everything in ourselves which is characteristically sound and original.

Mereschowsky has called him the great seer of the body, in contrast to Dostoiewsky, the seer of the soul. And truly the wholesomeness of Tolstoi's art rests upon its physicality. The psychological is already the pathological; the world of the soul is the world of disease, but the world of health is the world of the body. Tolstoi, of course, had no comprehension of Dostoiewsky, who wrote the best and profoundest critique of *Anna Karenina*, an exposition full of love and insight, strikingly recalling Schiller's large-hearted appreciation of *Wilhelm Meister*. When the author of *The Brothers Karamazov* died, Tolstoi for a moment fancied that he had "loved that man very much"; but he had never troubled about him in his lifetime, and the comments he made in conversation, upon Dostoiewsky's works, might have been uttered by any fool. He was diseased himself, he said, and made everything he touched diseased. Granted the truth of the words, it is an unworthy truth—as unworthy as to say of Nietzsche, "No, no, from the sick only sickness can come," which in this case would also be quite the opposite of the truth. Tolstoi's pronouncements were those of a great man, entirely arbitrary and irresponsible—one need only recall the time when he exalted *Uncle Tom's Cabin* above Shakespeare, and said that the latter was "immoral." Were his estimates of himself any more accurate? I leave out of consideration the period when he repudiated his titanic masterpiece as idle and sinful trifling. Much earlier than that, when he was writing *Anna Karenina*, the most powerful novel of social life ever penned, he flung aside the manuscript in disgust, not once but a dozen times, saying that it was utter rubbish. Even when it was done he said no better of it. We can hardly interpret this as merely a display of moody self-consciousness. He would not have let others so judge; and the measure he applied was one peculiar to himself alone. The true explanation of such self-depreciation by a great man and artist is that it arises out of an opinion of himself that far out-tops his performance. It may be true that a man must be greater than his work, and that the great must take rise from the greater. At least, such figures as Goethe, Lionardo and Tolstoi make one think so. But why did Tolstoi never once speak with like disdain of his sects and his doctrines, his theories of moral uplift, as he did of the creations of his art? Why did he never once crack a smile at them? The question is permissible—for if Tolstoi was greater than his works, surely he was greater than his thoughts!

Ah, yes, Tolstoi's views! They were harkened to like revelations, very likely because that was what they were: the autocratic utterances of the thing we call personality. They became right by main strength, by dint of that natural magic which turned into a shrine the manor-house in the province of Tula, making it a place of pilgrimage for human need, a centre whence power radiated into all the world. Vitality and greatness, greatness and power—how far are they one and the same thing? I am touching here on the problem of the "great man," that burning, unsettled question, puzzled over by humanity everywhere in the world. It has been answered by the Chinese democracy of reason in terms offensive to our ears, with the dictum that every great man is "a public calamity." The instinct of Europe is, and always has been, prepared to accept a justification of the phenomenon on æsthetic grounds. But if we mean by greatness leadership, edification, the lifting up of the level of humanity, then it is, to put it mildly, doubtful whether we can really ascribe such functions to the great man without somewhat wrenching the true cause the false way. Doubtful whether he does not rather represent a purely dynamic event, an explosion of power which is by its nature wholly indifferent to the moral sphere and quite pathetic in its attempts to give itself a moral significance—like the attempt made, with so much goodwill and so little natural capacity, by the prophet of Yasnaya Polyana, attended as that was by such embarrassment through the antics of his adepts. What a blessed life ! Blest—to the heights and the depths of tragedy and comedy—by power, and not by spirit. For even the moral sufferings and aspirations of this amazing life have a swollen, distended aspect, as though they were the manifestation of some great force. What lay at the heart of it all ? What, but the physical horror of death, as felt by an enormous vitality which, even in its apparently intellectual guise, was nothing but a radiation of life ! For we must tell the truth, without fear of belittling his greatness : the end, the famous retreat of the holy man from home and family, had about it as much of the animal's instinctive flight into solitude at the approach of death as it had of yearning after social and religious salvation.

But in all these thoughts, I am haunted by those fine and reverent lines that Goethe wrote of man :

> "*Denkt er immer sich ins Rechte,*
> *Ist er ewig schön und gross ?*"

What modesty, what an example lies in the effort of that creative power, which being endowed by nature "did not need it," to "think himself into rightness" for humanity's sake, and to put his life-force at the service of the humane ideal and the intellectual life ! No matter though Tolstoi's creative art suffered shipwreck a hundred times, wandering lost in regions of the childish, savage and fantastic ; his struggle and his suffering remain "eternally fine and great." They were the issue of a profoundly correct emotional insight. Tolstoi perceived the dawning of a time when life-enhancing art would not of itself suffice ; when the leading, illuminating and decisive spirit which is to unify and serve society must supersede the objective genius, and the ethical and intelligent rise above the irresponsibly lovely ; and never did he sin in the direction of his own native greatness, never did he claim the licence of his genius to function in the sense of confusion, reaction, atavism, evil ; but always, as far as he could, served in true humility the reasonable and the divine.

I called that exemplary. We are a small breed, we middle-European writers of to-day, by comparison with his like. But we should be past forgiveness, if we let anything, least of all fear of the contempt, the reproach and enmity of fools, prevent us from satisfying the demands of the time, the spiritual duty, each in and for his own people, honestly and straightforwardly "to think ourselves into rightness."

FREUD'S POSITION IN THE HISTORY OF MODERN THOUGHT

FREUD'S POSITION IN THE HISTORY OF MODERN THOUGHT

In a significant aphorism headed "The German Hostility to Enlightenment," Nietzsche discusses the cultural contribution made by German philosophers, historians and scientists in the first half of the nineteenth century, and points out that the general tendency of these thinkers and investigators was directed against enlightenment and against the social revolution—"which then, in gross miscomprehension, passed as their work." Reverence toward the existing order, he says, sought to translate itself into reverence for all that existed in the past, "only that heart and mind might be once more full, with no room left for the aims and reforms of the future." He tells how the cult of feeling was erected in place of the cult of reason; speaks of the glorious part—more effective than that of any artists of the word or thought—played by German musicians in the building of the temple; but, while fully acknowledging the many benefits to historical justice which flowed therefrom, he is largely unwilling to let the fact be lost sight of, that it was "in general no small danger," in the guise of full and final acknowledgment of the past, to press down knowledge below feeling and, in the words of Kant, to make a new path for faith by showing knowledge its limits. "The hour of this danger," wrote Nietzsche in 1880, "is past." One might breathe freely once more. Those very spirits which the Germans had once so eloquently invoked were in the long run most injurious to the aims of their invokers. "History, the understanding of origins and developments, sympathy with the past, the newly roused passion of emotion and perception, all these played for a while the role of useful partner to the obscurantist, fanatic, retrograde spirit. Then one day they put on another nature, and spreading their broad pinions soared above and beyond their one-time summoners, as new and more powerful genii of that very enlightenment against which they had been invoked." "This enlightenment," Nietzsche concludes, "it is now ours to carry on, undisturbed by the fact that there has been 'a great revolution' and then 'a great reaction' against it ; yes, that both still exist, being as they are but little waves compared with the real and great flood on which we float and wish to float."

The burning life conveyed by these words, their immediate and most refreshing relevancy to the present, will not be lost on anyone who reads them to-day, almost half a century after they were written. And such a one, if he be at pains to keep his gaze clear into the open future of humanity, undeceived by the daily ebb and flow of the little waves, undistracted by the self-assured clamour of the prophets and toadies of the hour, will hearken to them in grateful reverence for the masterly genius of Nietzsche. For whether we know it or not, it is at the feet of his overshadowing greatness that all our present literally lies, with its thinking, willing, believing and striving ; with its struggles and convulsions like a satyr play, an ignoble repetition in little of his intellectual life ; its wrangling over problems which, in him and by him, were long since dealt with in the grand style. For what else to-day are all our controversies in the sphere of the intellect but as it were a journalistic recoinage of that epoch-making war of his upon Wagner, itself so symbolic throughout of the conquest of romanticism in him and by him ?

We have all good reason to-day to ponder well upon reaction and progress, romanticism and enlightenment ; also we should have by now learned caution in the use of those terms—provided that what we are bent on is to understand, not merely to prevail in an argument. The sort of caution I mean is recommended in an early study by Nietzsche, in *Menschliches, Allzumenschliches*, called "Progress and Reaction." He refers to the appearance of certain powerful and irresistible spirits, who yet are reactionary and invoke a past epoch, as indicating that the new orientation is not yet strong enough to oppose them successfully. And he hails in particular Schopenhauer as one of these triumphant reversions of genius, in whose teaching the whole pre-scientific, mediæval Christian conception of the universe—notwithstanding the long-since achieved destruction of all Christian dogma—once more celebrates a rebirth. And with exemplary objectivity Nietzsche weighs the advantages to be drawn from such spirits. They force back our feeling for the time, he says, into the great old ways of viewing man and the world, to which no other path could so well conduct us ; and thereby are of inestimable benefit to history and historical fair-mindedness. The historical point of view of the enlightenment, Nietzsche says, was scarcely in a position to do justice to Christianity and its Asiatic kindred ; the metaphysics of Schopenhauer, drawn from the life-experience of reactionary genius, supplied the corrective ; and only after this just triumph might we once more raise the banner of enlightenment, inscribed with the names of Erasmus, Petrarch and Voltaire. "We have," says he, "turned reaction into progress."

What we have here is of course an earlier version of the aphorism in *Morgenröte*, which I quoted above. It is equally instructive upon the involved, double-faced and questionable nature of intellectual processes. Reaction as progress, progress as reaction, the interweaving of the two, is a continually recurring historical phenomenon. Luther's reformation regarded as the triumph of an idea—who is to pronounce whether it was reaction or progress ? It was progress and liberation, the German form of revolution, heralding the French, and also it was a relapse into the Middle Ages, an almost killing frost upon the tender intellectual spring of the renaissance; it was an interplay of both, a mixture of life, deed and personality, that cannot be come at at all by means of purely intellectual criteria. And Christianity itself—with its awful revival and reanimation of the primitive in religion, its atavistic mentality, its blood- and bond-meal of the flesh of the divine sacrifice—Christianity itself, however inestimably significant for the humanising of man, the refining of his soul and spirit; however great the capacity for growth which it displayed from its inception, one can easily understand that to civilised antiquity it must have seemed like a hideous relapse and reversion, in which, in the most literal sense, the bottom of the world had come uppermost!

That the very Christianity which Luther "reformed" was itself a reformation, a return to and reassertion of primitive religion; that indeed reformations by their very nature have little to do with progress, since they tend to re-establish the old and the oldest in an extremely conservative sense, and that at a time when the new is already present, though also to a certain extent in alliance with that new: these things became clear to me as I re-read of late some pages of Freud's *Totem and Taboo*, in which he treats of the totem feast and the very realistic conception of blood communion as identity of substance on which it rests—that earliest feast of mankind, that commemoration of the primeval crime of parricide "in which so many things—social organisations, ethical prohibitions, religion—had their beginning." And he traces back through the ages the identity of the totem feast with animal sacrifice, theanthropic human sacrifice and the Christian Eucharist, probing with careful, inexorable surgeon's probe this whole horrifying and culturally highly fecund morbid world of incest dread (*Inzestangst*) and murder remorse (*Mordreue*), and yearning for salvation (*Erlösungsdrang*) ; analysing and illuminating, until the mind passes at length from consideration of these primitive abominations from which religious feeling takes its rise, from reflections upon the deeply conservative nature of all reforms, to dwell upon the author himself, his position and affiliations in the history of thought.

As a delver into the depths, a researcher in the psychology of instinct, Freud unquestionably belongs with those writers of the nineteenth century who, be it as historians, critics, philosophers or archæologians, stand opposed to rationalism, intellectualism, classicism—in a word, to the belief in mind held by the eighteenth and somewhat also by the nineteenth century ; emphasising instead the night side of nature and the soul as the actually life-conditioning and life-giving element ; cherishing it, scientifically advancing it, representing in the most revolutionary sense the divinity of earth, the primacy of the unconscious, the pre-mental, the will, the passions, or, as Nietzsche says, the "feeling" above the "reason." I have used the word "revolutionary" in what seems a paradoxical and logically perverse sense; for we are used to associate the idea with the powers of light, with the emancipation of the understanding and with conceptions looking futurewards, whereas here the leading is in just the opposite direction. Backwards, is the cry: back into the night, the sacred primitive, the fore-known, the life-bearing; backwards into the romantical, prehistorical mother-womb. That is the language of reaction. But the emphasis is revolutionary. No matter what the field of intellectual activity—whether history, where Arndt, Görres and Grimm set up the idea of the primitive folk against that of humanity; or cultural critique, where Carus exalts the unconsciously shaping life-principle at the expense of the spirit, and Schopenhauer humbles the intellect far below the will, before prescribing to it a means of moral conversion and self-regeneration; or archæology, where from Zoega, Creuzer and Müller to Bachofen, the legalist of matriarchy, all sympathy goes out to the chthonic and the dæmonic, to night and death—in short, to a pre-olympic, primeval and earth-born religion, in significant antagonism to the classical cult of reason—in whatever field, in every field, the will is present to "force back our feeling into the great old ways of looking at man and the world"; always the idea of the sacred past and the fruitfulness of death is set over against the shallow and outworn idealistic optimism of the daylight cult of Apollo. Always that is the new, the revolutionary word ; and with militant ardour is asserted and emphasised the powerlessness of mind and reason by contrast with the forces marshalled in the depth of the soul, with the dynamic of passion, the irrational, the unconscious. The line continues to Klages, the rediscoverer and reviver of Bachofen, and to Spengler the pessimist historian—in other words, down to our day and our most modern lines of thought. And thus we have present opportunity to study this psychologically so strange concurrence of disbelief in mind and hostility to mind. For this insight into the feebleness of the reason and the intellect, their oft-proven incapacity to condition life, has not given rise to a wish to pity and protect their weakness. On the contrary, they are treated by this school of thought as though there were a danger that they might ever become too strong, that there could ever be too much of them on this earth ; the weakness of mind is one reason more to hate it, to make a religion of decrying it as the grave-digger of life.

It will escape nobody that we have here the same "hostility against enlightenment" which Nietzsche describes in his aphorism. The danger that is bound up with such activities, however fruitful in discoveries, with however much of genius in the performance, is, he thought, "thank God," over and gone. In the long run they too, and precisely they, had advantaged the very enlightenment against which their masters invoked them, as waves in the great flood that bears humanity onwards. And we—have we the same feeling, the same experience? Can we regard as happily past that danger to humanity to which Nietzsche referred? Yes, if we rise to the height of his vision and take into consideration our better knowledge of the main currents of life and of universal world-tendencies. But emphatically no, if we surrender to the impressions daily and hourly forced upon us.

The great nineteenth century—to revile and contemn which is one of the most tasteless of our literary fashions—was certainly not "romantic" in its first half alone. The decades of its second half, the truly bourgeois-liberal, Philistine, materialistic decades, with their monism and their natural science, are strewn with romantic elements and products of decadence; it is in them that the romantic is persistently regarded as an element of civic virtue, in them—and never to be lost sight of—that the art of Richard Wagner had its triumph; that art, great as the century itself, scored through with all its characteristic traits, weighed down with its instincts and worthy to serve as a symbol of the heroic war waged by Nietzsche, the dragon-slayer of his day, the herald of all the new and better things that struggle up to the light out of the anarchy and confusion of our time. A popular fiction abroad to-day would have it that the present moment in our intellectual history repeats the situation at the beginning of the nineteenth century; that in to-day's animosity towards mind, to-day's cult of the instinctive and the dynamic, that links up with Bachofen and romanticism, we are to envisage a genuinely revolutionary movement directed against the intellectualism and the rationalistic belief in progress of bygone decades—as though, for instance, the folk-idea, that romantic apanage of nationalism, were standing in battle array, as the new, the youthful imperative of the hour, against "backward humanity," against an encroaching cosmopolitanism! No, no, all that is quite indefensible, it must be characterised for what it is: a fiction born of the time in which we stand, at a point where mind leaves off and politics begins—a pernicious fiction, of which there will be more to say later on. And what about those decades of tepid humanitarianism, of deluded confidence in the power of reason, the revolutionary overthrow of which we have witnessed to-day? The world war, that gigantic explosion of unreason, in which the positive cosmopolitan powers of the time, the Church as well as Socialism, went down to defeat before the negative cosmopolitan power of imperialistic capital, the international nationalism—the world war, I repeat, would have been a strange termination to such an epoch. Once more, the nineteenth century was "romantic" not only in its first half but throughout, through all its decades; its pride of science was balanced, yes, outweighed by its pessimism, its musical bond with night and death, for the sake of which we love it and defend it against the contempt of a present not half its size. Nietzsche's quarrel with the Socratic hostility to instinct gratified our prophets of the unconscious, even while they feel that his psychological method debars him from true understanding of the myth and from finding his way about in the "holy twilight of primeval time"; but through Nietzsche down to our own time there flows the nineteenth-century stream of anti-rationalistic tendency—in some cases, indeed, not so much through him as over and beyond him. For it has literally happened that a fanatical editor of the *Mutterrecht* undertook to "measure Nietzsche by Bachofen"—an attempt to measure the much greater by the undoubtedly great but still immeasurably smaller, the presumptuous absurdity of which was immeasurable too!

I have laid it upon myself, not uninstructed in the intellectual complicatedness of all life, to use with great caution the terms "reaction" and "progress." The historical phenomenon which Nietzsche named "Reaction as Progress" puts the problem of revolution, a problem the conflicting and double nature of which is so confusing to all heads to-day—and particularly to youthful ones—that the most dead-and-buried ideas can successfully masquerade as the greatest novelty, and it becomes highly imperative to clear up the point of view and reduce it to a simplicity which may save us from its dangerous misuse. The whole thing depends on the attitude we take up, by temperament and intention, toward the past and the future. The revolutionary principle is simply the will towards the future, which Novalis called "the really better world." It is the principle of consciousness and recognition, leading to higher levels; the will and the urge to destroy—by means of lifting them into consciousness—all the premature apparent harmonies and pseudo-perfections of life, that rest upon uncertain and morally inadequate awareness; and by analysis, by psychology, through phases of solution which, from the point of view of cultural unity, must be designated as anarchy, but in which there is no pause and no retreat, no restoration, no tenable standing ground, to break a path to a free and genuine unity of existence, secured by conscious possession, to the culture of men developed to complete self-consciousness. The name of revolution belongs only to the will that leads futurewards by the path of consciousness and resolution. This is what youth must be told to-day. No teaching or incitement to the great "Back, back!" no zeal for the past for its own sake, can write the word upon its banner save for the open end of confusion. By which I do not mean that the revolutionary will knows nothing of the past or of the deeps. The contrary should be asserted. It must and will know much of them, be very thoroughly at home therein; if only these dark precincts do not allure it for their own sake, if only it does not make common cause with them to preserve the pseudo-religious and the sham-traditional, in short, out of reactionary instinct; but instead presses on as a liberator and enlightener into those *oubliettes* so full of horrors and of priceless treasures.

Assuming then as fundamental—I know of no other way—this conditioning of the will as reactionary or revolutionary, according as it faces to the past or to the future, it will be decidedly a wrong reading of the history of thought to consider German romanticism a reactionary, anti-intellectual movement. There is, indeed, within romanticism, an historic school which one might characterise as reactionary in the sense in which we are using the word. You find in it that fanatic worship of the night side, that Josef Görres complex of earth, folk, nature, death and past time, a world of thought and feeling possessing almost irresistible charm—but of which, Nietzsche to the contrary notwithstanding, it is not quite easy to think as peculiarly German, since a Frenchman, the nationalist Maurice Barrès, has most brilliantly, most recently, and in the grand style, presented to European attention the whole phenomenon of the chthonic world. Furthermore, history, by its very nature, is cast in a conservative mould of thought, it faces towards the past—it would be hard, surely, to find an historian possessed of revolutionary sympathies. But German romanticism is not—however disconcerting the statement may be to preconceived ideas—historically minded; it faces the future, so much so that one may call it the most revolutionary and radical of German intellectual movements. Novalis' characterisation of the future as "the really better world" supports my statement in the most general and decisive way; but there are also a hundred traits, doctrines and enthusiastic paradoxes of this school of thought, to which applies word for word what I have tried above to say about the nature of revolutions—and no wonder, since, freely confessed, it was derived from them. The thought and the poetry of the romantic movement are addressed to the task of widening the field of consciousness; and so keen was its leaders' sense of the irreligion and inhumanity of sheer dull conservatism, that even Wackenroder, the music-mad monk, could confess his horror of the "mischievous guilelessness, the frightful, equivocal, oracular obscurantism of music." This horror, this conscientious scruple, are romantic. It is romantic, when one sees in art not nature, let us say, but the reverse. In the duality of spirit and nature, whose fusion in the third kingdom hovers before the eyes of all romanticism as the goal of human nature, art is entirely relegated to the sphere of mind, being essentially and indubitably sense, consciousness, unity, purpose. Such was Novalis' meaning, when he called *Wilhelm Meister* "entirely a product of art, a work of the understanding," and romanticists have never otherwise conceived art than as the opposite pole of the instinctive, natural and unconscious. Romanticism, indeed, in its radical way, might easily have gone to the other extreme and failed to recognise that art must be both body and mind, that she is like Proserpina in belonging both to the powers of the underworld and the powers of light. But this intellectual perception of the new *étape*, of the modern, the up-to-date and the future, is of the essence of romanticism.

One thing only could mislead us as to the revolutionary character of German romanticism—namely, that it lacks, or displays only intermittently, the social-revolutionary phase ; that mind and spirit in their development have been content to manifest no zeal for political aims. But the political is latent in every intellectual position. That there is much of the French Revolution in Novalis' intellectual radicalism ; that the genius of two differing peoples can show corresponding traits—all that has been most happily recognised and discussed in Georg Brandes' essay on the romantic school in Germany. It is clear that revolution does not necessarily manifest itself as a cult of reason and intellectual enlightenment ; that enlightenment in the narrower, historical sense of the word may be only one intellectual technique among others, to apply in renewing and advancing life ; and that even with diametrically opposed methods, in all the wave-play of changing views and opinions, the great and general enlightenment can and will be served. This view, this large and trusting and enduring conviction is the one we must try to cling to and make our own, when we observe the hostility to the intellect which is characteristic of our time : the widespread, reigning, anti-idealistic and anti-intellectual determination to dispute the primacy of mind and reason, to pour scorn upon it as the most unfruitful of illusions, and to set the irrational and instinctive, the powers of darkness and the depths triumphantly in possession of their rights once more. It would be a rash critic who would give the name of romanticism to this temper of the time, which prevails to-day nearly everywhere, but most of all in Germany. No, for love of the intellect, passionate utopianism, orientation toward the future, conscious revolutionary spirit, are all far too distinctive characteristics of the German romantic movement to let its name be applicable here. And just as little as romanticism —to whose intellectual affinity with the French Revolution we have already referred—can be thought of as a pure revulsion against the eighteenth century and its classicism, just so little, or even less, is the present glorification of the irrational a pure reaction against the imputed shallowness of the nineteenth. An epoch whose second half was presided over by geniuses like Schopenhauer, Wagner, Bismarck and Nietzsche, may scarcely be thought of as a rationalistic and asthenic attenuation of living forces, so strong that it could evoke as its only possible reaction a re-formation of the myth and a renewed cult of the under-world. The relation of our own epoch to the one just past, with its melancholy, its problems and its tendencies, all on the grand scale, is even more involved than is that of the romantic movement to the eighteenth century. The anti-intellectual movement we are now witnessing, the contempt of reason, the hatred of enlightenment, is permeated and ameliorated by tendencies to a young belief in mind and a human and wholehearted will to reason—in short, by a neo-idealism which sets up a relationship between the twentieth century and the eighteenth, and which has more right than any idolatry of the instinct to feel itself in revolutionary opposition to the nineteenth century's misanthropy, pessimism and rationalism. I have no mind to consider certain humiliating fallacies of the nineteenth century as typical traits of that epoch; I deny that the Philistinism of the monistic enlightenment ever really held sway over its profounder elements. I am acquainted with those of its concomitants to which our modern irrationalism forms a genuine and needed corrective, and against which thought is happily in the field to-day. The confusion and narrowness of its specialisation, everywhere uninformed by ideas and remote from all deeper and higher human questionings, called into being a fruitful craving for conspectus and a broader sweep of inquiry. Its conceptual preoccupations, its critique, the hopeless austerity of its methods of research, are redeemed, or neutralised, by a new interest in the concrete, an attitude of research in which feeling, intuition, spiritual implications reassert their right, and art secures its position as a genuine instrument of knowledge—so that one may speak of science as restored to the sphere where genius operates, and of a new possibility of reuniting the conceptions of science and wisdom. All which is much too humanly gratifying to permit that any tincture of anti-rationalism or contempt for mind should apply to it the antagonistic conception of reaction. When the mistaken exclusiveness of the strict and correct scientific world administers a rebuff to a book like Dacque's *Urwelt, Sage und Menschheit* and bars its author from an academic career, there is no doubt on which side we should be found: on that of the book, which is genuine revolution, or on the side of the academic refusal—which after all has proved nothing. I do not insist on the single instance; but nothing is more certain than that the "inestimable gain" for justice and knowledge which Nietzsche ascribed to certain anti-rational ways of looking at the world and man (which, as he says, force our thoughts back) may also be laid to the credit of this new scientific spirit, whose methods of observation and research are not those of the rational enlightenment, but yet, being directed toward revolution and the future, will, I am sure of it, serve enlightenment in the humanly great sense of the world. If there can be talk here of a danger, that danger which Nietzsche saw bound up with such movements as tend to "press down knowledge below feeling" and so to serve the backward-shaping spirit, that danger lies only so far in the new science itself, as it seems to afford the opportunity of abuse by actual reaction, by the powers of reversion and retrogression which, without leave asked, enter into an impudent and dissembling alliance with it. That is the present and momentary danger. It is no danger, in the long run and to a long view ; but there is a chance of momentary bewilderment and the diversion of valuable forces from the aims of life and of the future.

I am speaking of a present-day source of mischief ; everybody can see that it is the conception of revolution by whose aid this mischief is bred—namely, by the reaction that usurps its place, wears it as a disguise, and succeeds so well in doing this that the straightforward sense of youth, not fortified against such tricks, can be beguiled into accepting the most outworn devices as new and promising novelties. As far, indeed, as the phenomenon and the trick itself are concerned, one may actually speak of a novelty. For there was nothing like it before, at least there was nothing like this carrying out to order and on the word of command. The shrinking from the onward march of life there has always been, the clinging to ideas of preservation and restoration, the pious and deliberate, melancholy and defiant fixation with the past, the sympathy with death, which is not incompatible with a high degree of intellectuality, often more than is possessed by all too blithe progressiveness, precisely because it knows what it wants and wants to be nothing else ; is not unaware that life condemns it, but deems itself subtler than life, and gets an ironic satisfaction out of its temper of proud and unwavering hopelessness. Such temperaments, such views of life, exist to-day : people, and products, whose conscious conservatism is by no means lacking in personal dignity. I have elsewhere explicitly commented on one such work, Hans Pfistner's *Palestrina*, a musical and dramatic confession of faith, rich in psychological interest, which is a classic expression of the attitude I have in mind, and as an intellectual performance overtops head and shoulders all other contemporary operatic works. It would be the sheerest Philistinism to preach life and progress to natures such as these, who with heads turned backwards, lost to time, are steadily living out the past in the present. There is no danger here, only the profoundest melancholy ; and the æsthetic standard is the only applicable one. But we have a right to feel impatience, and even aversion, when hostility to life puts on the garb of youth and the future, and so disguised begins to ply its dismal task.

I think it is in place to protest, to shed some light of criticism upon these activities. And I repeat, there is something new about this ambition of the old to clothe itself in the garments of the young. For the old was wont to insist upon its age and to rail in no uncertain terms against the new. To-day it puts on the colour of youth, and the doubtful light of a very early dawn helps on the deception. It may succeed in looking like revolution, partly because there is revolution actually afoot—a revolution against mind: a new science, a new knowledge of the depths, precisely that very intuitionalistic research which, in Nietzsche's words, seeks to "press down the reason below the feeling," which is the herald of the unconscious, of the senses, of the driving power of instinct—or whatever circumstances you choose to apply to dæmonic and natural forces, which arraigns "mind" in challenging and contemptuous language. And its words fall flatteringly upon the ear of those whose hostility to mind is of quite a different and incomparably more genuine kind; they seize upon this pessimism, justifiable and necessary as it is as an instrument in the task of reconstructing world and mankind upon deeper, firmer foundations, seize upon and turn it in their hands to a defeatism whose only interest is in the destruction of belief in all "forward-looking and reforming aims" and turning such belief into disrepute as identical with the bald and old-fashioned enlightenment of day before yesterday. For all this the true revolution cares nothing, seeing probably no reason why it should concern itself. But we have reason, we who see the encouragement their labours lend to the powers of darkness; reason, perhaps, to speak of "no small common danger."

Verily there is to-day no false and mock pious conservatism, no hatred and fear of the future, no cant or stupidity, no spirit of brutal reaction ; no invocation of the *status quo*, no demand for restoration and a turning back in the path of knowledge and self-enlightenment, but has felt itself strengthened by the sympathy with the irrational displayed by modern research ; has tried to establish contact with it, make use of its name, glibly to identify itself with it, above all, to make political capital out of it, to translate it into terms of social anti-revolution and thus to make crude reaction appear in the guise of revolution. Simplicity itself. And if mind is actually nothing at all but a feeble resistance to life, if nature, instinct, force are the be-all of the frame of this world, and if this is indeed the very latest and newest discovery, then of a truth the old is the new and the young, and all that came before and lies beneath the reason is the only gospel of salvation ; and he that speaks of ideas, of freedom, of justice, he understands not at all the signs of the times but associates himself with "backward humanity." Then every attempt to help the reason to triumph over the instincts—even bad instincts—is a crime against life ; for there are no bad instincts, if instinct itself, being chthonic, is sacred. Then only barren, reactionary intellectualism would seek to bridge the gap between reality and the position of the intellectual vanguard, or be concerned to relax the tension which to-day prevails, more dangerously than ever, between the two. Social ameliorations, sharing in the search of the day after new and healthier economic developments—that is all nothing but obsolete Marxian materialism ; sympathy with humaner aims, with the world's yearning after spiritual unity, is simply shallow internationalism, pacifistic sophistry. While in arms against all this outmoded ideological lumber, there stands in the revolutionary freshness of youth the dynamic principle, mindless nature, the folk-soul, hatred, war.

There we have reaction as revolution : the great retreat, dressed out in the uniform of the advance guard, the storming party. Who can fathom such vanity ? For vanity it is : the need of contact, the desire, even perversely, to be in alliance with life, never at any price to seem to oneself God-forsaken. And that is, at bottom, a considerable compliment to the revolutionary idea, one proof the more of its time-enforcing power. Even the dying feels that without it one does not count ; thus it calls itself revolutionary, much as in 1918 feudal conservatism raised the flag of a people's party.

And youth ? Is it really going to fall victim to this crude abuse of the new knowledge of the depths of mind, committed by our mind-haters ? It seems so. Or, rather, it seems so at some times and in some places. We are no longer strangers to the disheartening sight of youthful bodies in gay quickstep, songs issuing from young lips, arms flung in a Roman salute, wasting the fine flight of their youth upon hoary ideas. The confusion must mount, if youth goes on lending its biologic charms to age and the evils of age. But it is only an apparent confusion, an ephemeral illusion. The evils of age will not become good and beautiful because youth puts them on; would not become so if the tragedy came to pass that youth shed its blood for them. Such errors and misconceptions cannot stand, they are predestined to be called to order and set aside. And it would, I think, hasten the process were youth to employ itself upon a modern phenomenon of research, which more effectively than any other renders vain an attempt to misuse them to obscure the concept of revolution. I mean psychoanalysis.

We no longer, of course, refer to the theory of psychoanalysis as a recognised—or a disputed—therapeutic method. Long ago—and certainly to the surprise of its physician founder—it outgrew the domain of medicine and became a world-movement that has penetrated into all possible fields of intellect and science: history of religion, pre-history, research in literature and art, mythology and folklore, pedagogy, and so on, thanks to the zeal in elaboration and application of experts who have developed round the medical and psychiatrical kernel this atmosphere of influences—which might almost be compared to that which surrounds the personal work of Stefan George. But being by origin a technique of healing, it has preserved in the broader intellectual fields its physicianly character, its human and ethical urge to restore and to re-establish the human element in every distraction and distortion to which it is subject in life. Its profoundest expertise in morbid states is unmistakably at work not ultimately for the sake of disease and the depths, not, that is, with an interest hostile to reason ; but first and last, armed with all the advantages that have accrued from exploring the dark abysses, in the interest of healing and redemption, of "enlightenment" in the most humane sense of the word. It is, I think, the physicianly scope and intent of analysis that gives it a peculiar status within the scientific movement of our time.

It belongs to that movement—so much is clear. It lends, indeed, strength and spirit to a tendency which is loath to concede to mind much power to condition life. Its emphasis on the dæmonic in nature, its passion for investigating the night side of the soul, makes it as anti-rationalistic as any product of the new spirit that lies locked in victorious struggle with the mechanistic and materialistic elements of the nineteenth century. Revolutionary it is entirely in that sense. "As a psychoanalyst," Freud takes occasion to say in a little autobiographical sketch, "I must of course be more interested in affective than in intellectual phenomena ; more in the unconscious than in the conscious mental life." An extremely simple sentence, but full of meaning. The most striking thing about it is the calm allusion to "unconscious mental life." It is difficult to-day to conceive what a revolutionary affront to academic psychology and to all philosophic habits of thought the new science of psychoanalysis offered in that single phrase "unconscious mental processes." It sounded seditious in the fullest sense of the word, it was a frantic contradiction in terms—or, if it was not a contradiction, then it flung down the gauntlet to all existing psychology. The psychical and the conscious were ideas that belonged together: the phenomena of consciousness were the content of the psyche, and the unconscious psyche—that, it was to be hoped, was an absurdity in the way of nomenclature. The hope was not realised. Freud showed that the psyche is unconscious of itself, and that consciousness is only a property which may be present at the psychic process, but whose absence makes no difference to it. Upon this statement rests his theory of the neuroses ; for it asserted and proved the phenomenon of suppression, the preventing an impulse from reaching the consciousness and its transformation into the neurotic symptom —a piece of evidence the extra-therapeutic character of which and its universal significance were certainly not known to its discoverer—though they are known throughout the world to-day. It was revolutionary, this proof, entirely in the sense of the anti-rationalistic, anti-intellectualistic movement of our time, and would be closely related to it in any history of modern thought.

What makes psychoanalysis stand out from this

movement is the quality of its revolutionary character, which is decidedly something more than reaction. The unassuming sentence I have quoted above, with its "taking more interest in affective than in intellectual processes" gives rise to thoughts upon the psychology of interest, itself a subject not without its complications and dangers. It is easy for an interest to reach the point of solidarity and sympathy with its object; from which it readily goes on to agree with something of which it only, in the first instance, set out to demonstrate the bare existence. An interest is interesting in itself; one asks wherein it consists, on what grounds and to what end. One asks, for instance, about a predominating interest in the emotional, whether it is itself of an affective or of an intellectual nature. For in the former case, it entails glorification of its object—which an interest surely ought not to entail. Freud's interest as a scientist in the affective does not degenerate into a glorification of its object at the expense of the intellectual sphere. His antirationalism consists in seeing the actual superiority of the impulse over the mind, power for power; not at all in lying down and grovelling before that superiority, or in contempt for mind. It gives no occasion for confusion, nor is itself prey to any. Its interest in impulse is unmistakably and unchangeably not a subserviency which denies mind and clings to "nature"; on the contrary, it works in the interest of the triumph it envisages in the future for mind and reason ; it serves—I use the poor proscribed word in its largest sense, independent of the wave-play of the time—it serves "enlightenment." "We may," says Freud, "emphasise as often as we like the fact that intellect is powerless compared with impulse in human life—we shall be right. But after all there is something peculiar about this weakness, the voice of the intellect is low, but it rests not till it gets a hearing. In the end, after countless repulses, it gets one after all." Those are his words. And it would be hard to draw any comfort for reaction from a doctrine in which the primacy of reason is concisely stated to be "the psychological ideal."

The doctrine is revolutionary not alone from the scientific point of view and with reference to earlier methods of research. It is so in the most actual, unmistakable sense, the one least susceptible of misapplication. It is revolutionary by definition, in the sense of the word brought out by the German romantic movement. The touching thing is, that Freud went his hard way quite alone, quite independent, in his character as physician and natural scientist, unsupported by the encouragement which our literature might have given him, without the benefit of personal contact therewith. Perhaps it must always be so ; the driving-power of his work has undoubtedly been the greater for the lack. He did not know Nietzsche, in whose writing lightning flashes of Freudian conceptions are everywhere to be found. It is almost more to be regretted that he did not know Novalis, if we grant that it would have been good had his path been smoother. But perhaps our very subject, the psychology of the unconscious, will excuse us for suggesting unconscious influences, the working of a supra-personal transmission of ideas.

There is a kind of relationship that does not imply dependency; and such is the nature of the remarkable relation between Freud and the German romanticists. The signs of it are almost more striking than those of his unconscious derivation from Nietzsche, though they have as yet scarcely been noticed. When, for instance, Freud says that the primary human impulse is to return to the lifeless; when he seeks to solve the problem of impulse entirely by comprehending within the conception "Eros" "the preservation of self and the preservation of the species," opposing to it "the silently working urge to death or destruction" and "conceives impulse, generally speaking, as a sort of elastic property of life, an urge to reconstitute a situation which has once existed and been destroyed by outward influences"; when he speaks of the *essentially conservative nature of impulse* and defines life as the play and interplay of Eros and the death urge, all that sounds like a paraphrase of Novalis' aphorism: "The tendency of the elements that compose us is towards de-oxidisation. Life is forced oxidisation." Novalis too sees in all-embracing Eros the principle that urges the organic to ever-increasing unity, and the erotic radicalism of his social psychology is a mystic prefiguration of Freud's discoveries and speculations on the natural-science side. "Amor it is that presses us together"; thus Novalis. And when Freud speaks of a narcissistic libido of the ego and derives it from the products of the libido which holds the body cells together, the idea is such a romantic-biologic speculation that its absence from the writings of Novalis would seem to be due to mere chance.

What has been falsely called Freud's pan-sexualism, his theory of the libido, is, to put it briefly, nothing but natural science divested of mysticism and become romanticism. This it is has made of him a psychologist of the depths, an investigator of the unconscious, that makes him understand life through disease; that gives him his place in the anti-rationalist scientific movement of to-day—and also distinguishes him from it. For there is an intellectual ingredient in the theory that makes it impossible to use it in any practically reactionary sense; that confines its anti-intellectualism to the realm of knowledge and gives it no power to encroach upon the will. And this intellectuality is bound up with the very theory the predominance of which has roused the greatest hostility to his whole teaching—because the prepossessions of Christianity have accustomed us to regard it as something sinful and impure—I mean, of course, the idea of sex. When he describes the impulse to death and destruction as the effort of the living to relax the strain by returning to lifelessness, and then crosses this backward urge with the "actual life-impulse," namely sex, with which all striving toward evolution, fulfilment and unification is bound up, he gives to sexuality a revolutionary and intellectual significance which Christianity has been very far from ascribing to it.

We are familiar with the extent to which Freud's whole cultural psychology is based upon the fatality of impulse, and with the rôle which the conceptions of sublimation and suppression play in it. And here we have the root of the socialism that comes out clearly in more than one place in his writings—here, in his theory of the neuroses. We know that for him the neurotic symptom is the consequence—not the inevitable, but precisely the pathological consequence of suppression. Looked at from this point of view, it is plain that he regards our whole culture as standing in the sign and image of the substitution-neurosis—understood as much more than an illustration and a simile, and in good part as quite literally and actually, though reaching out beyond the literal application. Freud sees in our civilisation an apparent harmony, an apparent completeness, which is really very unstable, very insecure; similar—and not only similar—to the state in which a neurotic patient, without a will to recovery, comes to terms with his symptoms; "a state of existence," he says, "which neither can nor deserves to continue." And here begins the extraordinary relationship, so important for the history of thought, between his teaching and the philosophy of the becoming-conscious, represented by Novalis. It displays the same romantic sensitiveness for all the inhumanity of sheer dull conservatism, for the bigotry which would, at whatever cost, preserve premature, morally inadequate forms of life, based upon the lack of self-consciousness. It indicates the dissolution of such immature forms, to be brought about by critical vision ; it believes, like romanticism, in the transcendence of disorder, in ever higher stages, and in the future. The way which it prescribes is that of increasing consciousness, of analysis ; upon it there is no retreat, no reversion to the good old times ; its goal is a new life-order, earned by effort, resting on freedom and security, secured by self-knowledge. Measured by its method and its aims it may be said to tend to enlightenment, but of a kind too disciplined to be open to any charges of blithe superficiality. It might be called anti-rational, since it deals, in the interests of research, with the night, the dream, impulse, the pre-rational ; and the concept of the unconscious presides at its beginnings. But it is far from letting those interests make it a tool of the obscurantist, fanatic, backward-shaping spirit. It is that manifestation of modern irrationalism which stands unequivocally firm against all reactionary misuse. It is, in my sincere conviction, one of the great foundation-stones to a structure of the future which shall be the dwelling-place of a free and conscious humanity.

CULTURE AND SOCIALISM

CULTURE AND SOCIALISM

It is pure nonsense—or perhaps not so pure either—of which our political philologians are guilty, when they accuse me of falsifying my book, *The Reflections of an Unpolitical Man*, and disingenuously turning a piece of anti-democratic propaganda into a democratic tract, simply because in the year 1922 I relieved of a few not very tenable pages the cumbersome product of those unforgettable years of suffering, and thus saved it from going into two volumes in the collected edition of my works. I am far too conscious of this book as a record of my personal experience and that of the time, to be able to lay a hand on it in the way of altering the views it expresses; and nobody can with justice complain that the product of irritation against a democratic and anti-German propaganda of righteousness, which is to-day just as repellent to me as it ever was, offers less handle to misuse as a part of my collected works than it did when it first appeared. The product of that long and tortured intellectual burrowing into the character and destiny of Germany remains what it was: an arsenal of embittered ammunition—if not against democracy, then against what is understood by the word. Indeed, a more justifiable reproach than the one which has been levelled might be, that I had no right to include in my collected works a book which was once helpful to many, but whose views I had most bewilderingly repudiated in later utterances which were likewise included in the collected edition.

But this objection is not tenable either. For I do not repudiate the *Reflections*, nor have I ever done so by a single subsequent word. One does not repudiate one's life, one's experiences ; one does not repudiate what one has "gone through"—precisely because one has gone through it, and, if not essentially, still in intention, come out a little farther on than one went in. Collected works are spiritual autobiographies, which may, and must, exhibit the steps and stages of the inner life, raised by dint of form to relatively final permanence and validity, though not for that reason static ; and what we have gone through is proportionately dearer to us in retrospect, the more passion, the more of our heart's blood we have devoted to it when it was the inmost present of our existence. The *Reflections* are the product of long, deep, painful devotion to a problem which at the time had become the most utterly personal and pressing, the problem of the German genius—and is it likely I would disclaim it ? Did it, think you, escape me, that this book is worth far more, artistically speaking, as a literary performance, with all the melancholy of its mood, than the fatherly admonishment to a republic with which a few years later the author surprised refractory youth ? The latter was the expression of a cordial acceptance of life, the earlier of a sympathy with death, and both legitimate concomitants of the writer's nature. If the *Reflections* was not a work of art, at least it was the work of an artist, and an artist who was bent on understanding and on nothing else. Understanding, however, for an artist, is to be had in no other way than by self-devotion, by the route of passion, by loving absorption into his subject ; and thus the impassioned critique of the German genius which forms the subject-matter of the book, took on the assertive, belligerently apologetic tone so offensive to the intellectual life of the time. That life saw in it a betrayal and a cheap submission, an ordinary hunting with the hounds. Precisely that it was not, that voluminous rescript of suffering ! It did not, it refused to hunt with the hounds. It looked back ; it went on record in defence of a great intellectual past. It was bent on being a monument ; if I mistake not it has become one. It was a rear-guard action, in the grand style, the latest and last of German middle-class romanticism ; fought in full consciousness that it was a lost cause and thus not without greatness of soul ; fought, indeed, with insight into the mental unhealthiness and viciousness of all sympathy with the *fey* ; yet also, it is true, with æsthetic, too æsthetic contempt of health and virtue, which were felt—and scorned—as the sum and essence of that before which one retreated fighting: politics, democracy.

The intellect should be objective enough to admit that it makes no difference whether a perception is positive or negative in sense, provided it is a perception and a true one. The activistic spirit itself, against which, with a great sense of freedom, the *Reflections* stoutly inveighs, would admit this position when it is a matter of national self-knowledge. And also when it happens "on its own account," or even in the sense of an apologia; there is no self-knowledge that leaves its object—that is to say, its subject—untouched, that does not issue in change, does not have consequences, precisely as the activistic spirit demands. As I have elsewhere said: we underestimate self-knowledge, calling it idle, quietistic, pietistic. But nobody remains quite what he is, when he knows himself. So much the *Reflections* has taught—to the indignation of those who were concerned not with the ideas but with the opinions and prophecies therein expressed. I am not wedded to the opinions. But the ideas remain incontestably correct; and the problem, the German problem, the problem of the German nation, which I took upon myself to tilt at, has since then lost not a jot of its burning timeliness.

What, then, was the fundamental idea of the book, the axiom which formed its point of departure? It was the identity of politics and democracy, and the essential un-Germanness of the combination; in other words, the native strangeness of the German spirit towards the world of politics or democracy, against which it sets up, as its own peculiar concept, the unpolitical, aristocratic one of culture. The feeling was obscure, yet incontestable, that this strangeness and refractoriness were at bottom the cause of the war; that it was through them that Germany became isolated and they that roused up the world in arms against us. German *Kultur*! In 1914 there was nothing in the world more hated, more reviled—and that it was spelt with a *K* was to *entente* journalists an added source of embitterment. But the unbridled animosity of the enemy world against this capital k need not surprise us. That it stung us and spurred us on to defend our own is understandable; but laugh it aside we might not and could not, for the conception of *Kultur* stood at the heart of our war ideology, just as at the heart of the enemy's stood the politico-democratic notion of "civilisation." We were thus entirely at one with the enemy as to the only possible spiritual basis for such a war—and doubtless we were both right. But aside from the grounds on which the war became spiritually possible, and on which it could be spiritually fought, there was also the war as a prosaic reality, with all its highly unspiritual origins, interests and aims; and that its ideology could so blind the German citizen as to its other, actual and brutal side, hung together with the non-political idealism, the uncritical simple-mindedness of his conception of culture; this, he felt, was sacrosanct; it was laid upon him to defend it with all the destructive resources of all his munition factories.

The war was lost. But what most shattered the German's morale was not the physical defeat, the ruin, the tremendous plunge into national humiliation from the height of outward power. It was a more frightful derangement still: it was the profanation of his faith, the defeat of his idea, the crash of his ideology, the catastrophe to the cultural ideal which was that ideology's centre of power—it was this that had been defeated in the defeat, and the victor was the opposed pole of the idea, the world of democratic civilisation. Germany had engaged herself far too deeply in the realm of dialectics, in the field of theory, not to be overwhelmed with the conviction that she had suffered a downfall of the idea; and her desperate attempts to deny her defeat, her protests that she was "unconquered in the field" took place on ideological grounds—she hoped thereby to deny her intellectual, her so to speak philosophical, defeat as well. The conflicts that rend Germany to-day wear many names and take many shapes. But at bottom they are one: the conflict between defiance and the will to compromise; the grim, embittered question, shall Germany abide by her traditional conception of culture, or lay hand upon it to transmute it into the new? We are too intellectual a people to be able to live under a conflict between our faith and our polity. When she introduced the republican forms, Germany was not "democratised." All German conservatism, all sincere belief that the traditional German idea must be left untouched, must, in the political sphere, repudiate the republican, the democratic form of government as foreign to land and folk, as false and intellectually repugnant to the realistic sense. That lies in the nature and inward consistency of things ; as, similarly, only those can support the democratic form and have faith in its viability in the Germany of the future, who consider that the transformation of the German cultural idea in a world-reconciling, democratic sense, is both possible and desirable.

It ought to be said that the actual, essential difficulties in the way of the democratisation of Germany are little understood abroad, and all our efforts to set the wheels in motion are insufficiently appreciated. People wonder at our false starts ; they are strengthened in their political mistrust—they overlook the fact that almost all the intellectual preconditions for success are lacking. The framers and teachers of German humanism—the Luthers, Goethes, Schopenhauers, Nietzsches, Georges—were no democrats. Oh, no. If their names are honoured outside our borders, let those who honour them realise what they do. It was they who created the *Kultur* with the big *K* that formed the power centre of German war ideology. In Paris they applaud the *Meistersinger*. That is to misinterpret the association of ideas. For of the *Meistersinger* Nietzsche wrote : "Against civilisation. The German against the French."

The word culture is of one origin with the word cult. Both mean care : the one in the sense of reverence for, and ritual attendance on, the articles of salvation ; the other in the sense of a purely human, æsthetic and ethical refinement, divorced from the religious—an ennobling, an enhancement of the individual, a process which, without directly aiming at it, is supposed to advantage the world at large. And just there, in the involuntariness and personal unawareness of the individual as to its super- and extra-individual bearing, there enters into the conception an element of the marvellous and mythical which re-emphasises its near-religious character. For "culture" is, contrasted with cult, a secular conception ; but coupled with the idea of civilisation, it reveals its religious, in other words, its essentially unsocial, egotistically individualistic character. "The religious man," says Nietzsche, "thinks only of himself." That is, he thinks of his deliverance, the salvation of his soul, and, originally, at least, of nothing else ; yet privately he pays homage to the faith, and trusts in the promise, that the inward working of his own salvation will in some mystical way redound to the salvation of the whole. And the same is altogether the case of the believer in culture.

But the human race dwells in common on this

earth, and there is no isolation, no immediacy with God, to which would not correspond some form of association and social community. The religious ego becomes corporative in the communion. The cultural ego celebrates its highest feasts in the form of and under the name of the community—a strongly aristocratic word, with a stress upon the cultural element, that distinguishes the religious character of its social idea from the secular conception of society which belongs to a democratic civilisation. Most instructive for the distinction between "community" and "society"—between the cultural and the democratic structure—I have always found the institution of the theatre. It is an institution native to every country, yet in every country bears its individual stamp. When I was twenty years old I spent a year in Italy. When I returned to my native land the most German, the most indigenous thing I found there, was the cultural discipline that dominates the German theatre. This by contrast with the social laxity which marked the performances I had seen abroad. The German theatre is at bottom bound up with the cult- and cultural-idea of the community; from that sphere it draws the metaphysical value, the positive character of its place in society, the intellectual seriousness which its creators and poets have stamped upon it—of all of which the theatre of the West and the South is almost entirely unaware. For the latter is a tribune, a forum, a newspaper, an instrument for the analysis and current critique of public events; whereas the German theatre is a temple. Ideally, I mean. As for its audience, it is the *folk*—again because their masters will it and the idea triumphs over the empirical; whereas in the other theatre the audience is the social group, and in the highest and most solemn contingencies the nation. In the distinction I am making nobody can fail to hear the romantic ring, the aristocratic simplicity of the word folk, the expression "*das deutsche Volk*" contrasted with the word nation, and the democratic, revolutionary associations the latter implies. It is actually false to speak of a nation of Germans, and well-nigh absurd that in Germany the people who are against democracy are called "German-national." Our Peoples' parties are better advised, linguistically speaking, whatever one's attitude otherwise toward their alarming smugness. For the conception "nation" is historically bound up with the idea of democracy, whereas the word "folk" corresponds to the actual German—that is to say, culturally conservative, non-political, anti-society idea, and our political romanticists, Constantin Frantz and Bogumil Goltz, contended on good grounds that Germany never has been a nation.

The difficulties in the way of a real, intrinsic and not merely legal democratisation of Germany I have here tried if not to exhibit at least in some measure to suggest. It goes without saying that they are closely related to the folk-idea, the conception of culture, and take their rise therefrom. If to-day we are confronted by the tragi-comic phenomenon that in Germany to-day, in this culture-worshipping, non- and anti-political country, everybody plays and is driven to play politics, the reason is that it is no longer possible to draw a line between culture-politics and political politics ; that all culture-politics is already politics in the sense of the word most repellent to the feeling, and all such politics in fact culture-politics ; that all partisan activity in Germany is oriented according to a partisan conception of culture and conditioned by the question whether the attitude one takes up is conservative or to some extent liberal. But to what extent the word liberal is here used only in the sense of an intellectual two-party system, not in that of a parliamentary centre and middle-class position, becomes clear when I add that what we are really dealing with is socialism.

German socialism, the invention of a Jewish social theorist brought up in western Europe, has always, in the mind of the culturally conservative German, been considered foreign to the country and antagonistic to the people, as the devil's work pure and simple, and cursed accordingly ; with good reason, for it means the dissolution of the cultural, the anti-social folk- and community-idea, and its replacement by that of the social class. This process of dissolution is, in fact, so far advanced, that the cultural complex of ideas contained in the words folk and community must to-day be considered to be purely romantic. Life, with all that it holds of present and future, is beyond any doubt on the side of socialism. No mind turned lifewards—be it only on deliberately moral grounds, and without reference to its romantic and perhaps death-bound nature—but is driven to side with it and not with the party of bourgeois culture. And the reason is this: that whereas originally the intellectual, in the shape of individualistic idealism, was bound up with the conception of culture, while the social concept, the class idea, never denied its purely economic origins, it is in these days the latter that entertains toward the things of the mind far friendlier feelings than do its folk- and middle-class opponents, whose conservatism has almost lost touch with the living spirit and its patent claims. I have, and not long ago, referred to the morbid and dangerous state of tension which has been set up in the world between the spirit, the height which the peak of humanity has already reached and made its own, and material reality and the state of enlightenment thought to be possible and attainable therein. It is the Socialists, the workers, who display an undoubtedly stronger and more vital will toward the relaxing of this humiliating and dangerous tension than do their cultural opponents; whether the field be legislation, the nationalisation of the life of the state, the international constitution of Europe, or whatever you like. The socialist class, in direct opposition to the cultural, is, in economic theory, alien to intellect, but in practice friendly to it—and that, as matters stand to-day, is decisive.

The actual inadequacy of traditional intellectualism in Germany, its powerlessness to aid the mind turned futurewards—however strong the bond which the latter feels with it—is due to the fact that traditional intellectualism lacks the social, the socialistic ingredient. Nietzsche lacks it, and by consequence Stefan George, the burden of whose lay deals wholly with the folk-cultural, the romantic and communal, and displays toward the social idea all the rigid and lofty elegance which characterises his æsthetic position as a whole. Not that this great writer denies thereby his descent from Parnassus and from æstheticism. But æstheticism, bound up with the cultural ideal and—as pure individualism—with the conception of union held by the romantic folk-community, ignores and disclaims the German problem. And that problem consists precisely in the question at issue, with reference to which the parties are aligned: whether the social is to be interpreted culturally, according to the traditional conservative position, or politically—in other words, according to the socialistic conception of society. The translation of the folk idea into politics, the transposition of the community conception into the social and socialistic, will mean the real, inward and spiritual democratisation of Germany.

Thus, then, whoever in Germany to-day speaks of "democracy" does not mean the rabble, the corruption and party wire-pulling that popularly go by that name ; rather he speaks in the sense of recommending to the cultural ideal far-reaching concessions to the socialistic conception of society—which of a truth has long since triumphed, and will soon make an end of the cultural conception if it refuses to bow to the inevitable. Those who love it for the sake of its great past can but say what it must needs hear ; can but set before its eyes the certain and already consummated victory of Socialist opposition, and demand from it flexibility, goodwill, receptivity, fresh perceptions—without themselves being labelled as politically radical thereby. For political radicalism is a surrender to the communist doctrine of salvation ; it involves a faith in the saving grace of the social idea of the proletariat, which, when all is said and done, as little deserves it as does the cultural idea. It is a faith in the salvation of man by his own power, only tenable in a state of fanatical self-hypnosis. What would be needed, what would after all be typically German, would be an alliance, a compact between the conservative culture-idea and revolutionary social thought : to put it pointedly, as I have elsewhere done once before, an understanding between Greece and Moscow. It would be well with Germany, I repeat, she would have found herself, as soon as Karl Marx shall have read Friedrich Hölderlin. Such a contact, moreover, is about to be established. But I must add, that if it is one-sided it will bear no fruit.

ON THE THEORY OF SPENGLER

ON THE THEORY OF SPENGLER

Nietzsche once remarked that the saying "A prophet is not without honour save in his own country" is false, the contrary, in fact, being the truth. By which he probably means that nobody attains to fame abroad who has not first achieved it at home. Certainly in this form the dictum is applicable to Oswald Spengler's great work with the stark and catastrophic title, *The Decline of the West*: it has won world-wide popularity on the basis of the extraordinary success it has had in Germany—a success the more significant in that the book is not fiction, not a novel in the usual sense of the word, but a profound philosophical work, with the alarmingly learned sub-title: "Attempt to construct a morphology of the history of the world." Whatever one's mental reservations, one may regard with national gratification a success to which conditions here in Germany to-day have contributed as perhaps nowhere else in the world.

We are an uprooted folk. The cataclysms that have gone over our heads: the war, the unbelievable downfall of a government that seemed *aere perennius*, the radical restratifications, both economic and social —in short, a succession of storms have put us as a nation in a state of tension to which we had long been strangers. And all over the world the things of the mind are in a condition to heighten the tension. Everything is in flux. The natural sciences, which at the turn of the century seemed to have nothing to do but to confirm and amplify their previous achievements, are now facing a new era, so fantastic, so revolutionary in character as to make the researcher's head reel, and cause wide repercussions in the lay world. The arts lie locked in a crisis which seems at times to be a mortal one, at times to portend the birth of new forms. Our problems flow together, one cannot keep them separate, cannot be a politician without knowledge of the things of the mind, nor remain æsthete—"pure artist"—while being gnawed at by all the worries of the socially conscious. The problem of man himself, the human being, never looked more threatening, more challenging than it does to-day in the eyes of serious people; what wonder that it bears most heavily on, urges most immediately to action those who are prostrated, those who are most acutely conscious that the world and our time are facing portentous change? Since 1914 there has been much discussion in Germany, discussion so boundless as to be almost Russian: if that statesman was right who said "Democracy is discussion," then truly we are a democratic people.

We read avidly. Not for diversion or distraction,

but for truth's sake and the arming of our minds. The public has quite visibly lost interest in belles-lettres in the narrow sense, in favour of the critical, the philosophical, in short, the intellectual. Or, better expressed, there has largely taken place that fusion of the spheres of criticism and creation, which was inaugurated by our romantic school and powerfully furthered by the appearance of that mixture of learning and lyricism which we know as Nietzsche. And in the process the boundaries between science and art have been obliterated ; fresh blood flows through the ideas and reanimates the form, producing a type of book which rules to-day—a product which might be called a novel of the intellect. To this genre belong *The Travel Diary of a Philosopher*, the fine book on Nietzsche by Ernst Bertram and the monumental *Goethe* by Gundolf, the prophet of George. And by right of its literary brilliance and the mingled rhapsody and intuition he displays in his portrayal of civilisations and epochs, Spengler's *Decline of the West* indubitably belongs to this class. Its appeal was far and away the most sensational of them all, reinforced as it was by the "wave of historic pessimism" which, in Croce's phrase, is sweeping over Germany to-day.

Spengler denies that he is a pessimist. Still less, I suppose, would he call himself an optimist. He is a fatalist. But his fatalism, summed up in the sentence, "We must will the inevitable or nothing," is far from having the tragic, the heroic, the dionysiac character possessed by Nietzsche's resolution of the contradiction between optimism and pessimism. Rather it is a malicious demonstration of hostility to the future, in the disguise of scientific ruthlessness. It is not *amor fati*—indeed with *amor* of any kind it has little to do ; that is the repellent thing about it. Neither pessimism nor optimism is in question. Though we may envisage but darkly the fate of mankind, thinking it doomed to suffer through endless ages ; though we may shroud ourselves in the profoundest scepticism and refuse to believe in any hypothetic future happiness ; yet we shall not thereby relish the more, by a single grain, the schoolmasterish insensibility of the Spenglerian brand of pessimism. Pessimism is not lovelessness. It does not necessarily mean a cold-blooded, "scientific" mastery over the forces of evolution and a contemptuous disregard of such imponderabilia as are manifested by the spirit and the will of man, since these perhaps add to the process an element of irrationality not accessible to scientific calculation. But such presumption, and such disregard of the human element, are what Spengler represents. He might be as cynical as the devil himself—but no, he is only fatalist. And it is ill done of him to speak of Goethe, Nietzsche and Schopenhauer as the forerunners of his own hyenalike gift of prophecy. For they were human beings, while he is a defeatist of humanity.

I assume that my readers have read the *Decline*

of the West: I can do so confidently, for it has achieved world-wide reputation, due to certain great characteristics; nobody would dispute its possession of these. Its theory, in a nutshell, is this: what we call history is the life-course of certain vegetative and structurally similar organisms, each possessing its own span of life and its own individual characteristics. Each of these is a "culture." So far there have been eight of them: the Egyptian, Indian, Babylonian, Chinese, "classical," Arabic, Occidental (our own) and the Mayan (Central American). But though alike in their general structure and their common fate, these cultures are strictly self-contained forms of life; each inevitably committed to its own laws of style, in all its thinking, seeing, feeling, living—and each quite shut off from all understanding of the others. Herr Spengler, and he alone, understands all of them; he knows what to say about one and all in a way that is a joy to hear. Otherwise, as I have said, there reigns a profound lack of mutual understanding. Sheer absurdity to speak of a continuity of life, of ultimate spiritual unity, of that humanity which, according to Novalis, is the higher meaning of our planet, the star that links us with the upper world, the eye it lifts to heaven. Vain to remind oneself that a single work of love—like Mahler's "Song of the Earth," which takes an old-Chinese lyric and fuses it into an organic human unity with the most developed tonal art of the West—knocks into a cocked hat this whole conception of the essential unrelatedness between civilisations! Since there is no humanity, there is, according to Spengler, likewise no mathematics, no art of painting, no physics; there are only as many mathematics, physics and arts of painting as there are cultures; and these are essentially disparate things. There reigns a Babylonian confusion of tongues; but Herr Spengler again, endowed with the gift of intuition, can understand them all. Each culture, he says, has a span of life like a human being. Born of its parent landscape, each blossoms, ripens, fades and dies. Dies, after it has manifested its characteristics, exhausted all the possibilities of picturesque expression with which it was endowed—such as nationalities, religions, literatures, arts, sciences, forms of government. And the grey old age of each, its transition into nothingness and the rigor mortis of no-history, that is what we know as civilisation. But since any stage of a given culture can be deduced from all the others, we have in the first place a new and diverting conception of contemporaneity, and in the second—for people in the know—an astronomical certainty of what is going to happen. Take, for instance, our own culture, the occidental—which at the beginning of the nineteenth century entered the old-age phase of "civilisation," and whose immediate future will be "contemporaneous" with the century of the Roman soldier-emperors—its course is quite fixed. Astronomically, biologically, morphologically fixed. Appallingly fixed. And if there is anything more appalling than fate, it is the human being who bears it without lifting a finger.

This to do is what the adamantine scholar admonishes us. We must, he says, will the inevitable or nothing ; heedless that that is no alternative ; that man, by willing only that which inexorable science says must be, simply ceases to will—which is after all not precisely human. And this inevitable —what is it ? It is the decline of the west. That is the writing on the wall : a decline not precisely in so many words, not in the material sense, though much material decline will be bound up with it ; but the decline of the occident as a culture. China still exists, and many millions of Chinese, but the Chinese culture is dead. So it is with Egypt : since Roman times it is no longer occupied by an indigenous cultural population but by fellaheen. And the fellaheen state is, so Spengler says, the final condition of all folk life. When its culture has lived itself out a people passes into the fellaheen stage ; it reverts to its primitive, unhistoried condition. But the intellectual, political and economical instrument of this result is civilisation. It is the spirit of the city : it brings on the conception of the fourth estate, the masses ; and these masses, the nomads of the big city, are no longer the people, they are formlessness, the end, nothingness. For the west, as for every culture, the rise of formless, traditional forces (Napoleon) coincides with the beginning of civilisation. But Napoleonism passes into Caesarism, the parliamentary democracy into the dictatorship of single individuals of power and race, unscrupulous economic conquistadors of the type of Cecil Rhodes. The Caesarist stage is a feature of all declining cultures and lasts all of two centuries. In China it is called "the time of the fighting states." This is our own stage. At the beginning of the twentieth century private power as a political force succeeded the power of parliamentary parties, these being always conditioned by abstract ideals. The personal power, the single great man, rules over nerveless multitudes of fellaheen, which he treats like cattle. Another Caesar can always rise—another Goethe never ; and it is sheer flabby sentimentality to spend any time to-day on cultural affairs—art, poetry, education. Such things are not for fellaheen. The literary life of to-day has no significance whatever save as a futile struggle between the intellectualised art of the cities and the backward, idyllic art of the soil. He who grasps the forces of destiny will pay no heed to such trifles ; he will cling to those things which are all the future has and is : to the machine, technique, economics, and perhaps still politics. Laughter is the portion of those who believe in good-will and flatter themselves that goodness, spirit and will belong to a worthier order of mankind, that they too might have some influence over the course of our world. What is to come is fixed : wars on the vastest scale for power and plunder ; rivers of blood ; for the fellaheen populations, silence and submission.

Man, relapsed into the cosmic, zoologic, post-historied, will live as a peasant bound to the soil, or dully grubbing among the ruins of cities. To lull his suffering soul he will produce the so-called "second state of religion," a substitute for his earlier cultural and creative kind, with just effectiveness enough to help him bear his sufferings with resignation.

The man who possesses this refreshing outlook on life is a peculiarly puzzling phenomenon. His theory is cold, scientific, emotionless, lifted above all human prejudice ; relentlessly deterministic ; it seems to be pure knowledge. Yet through it is manifest a will, a conception of the world, sympathies and antipathies ; it is then at bottom *not* emotionless, it is secretly conservative. For one does not set up a creed of this kind, does not so marshal his facts, so identify history and culture, so sharply emphasise the antithesis between form and spirit, unless he is a conservative, unless in his heart he accepts form and culture and shudders at the decay of civilisation. The complexity and the perversity of the Spengler position consists—or seems to consist—in that despite this second, secret conservatism he does not affirm culture, does not like a preacher threaten death and decay in order to ward them off, but, on the contrary, affirms "civilisation," wilfully accepts it with a kind of fatalistic fury, and with ruthless scorn takes its side against culture, because forsooth the future belongs to it, and all that is cultural is doomed to death. To such cruel self-conquest and self-denial the stern heroic thinker goads himself on. Secretly conservative, a man of culture, he seems to be affirming civilisation only in a contrary spirit ; but no, that is only the seeming of a seeming, a double delusion ; for he is genuinely affirming it—not only with his words, against which his being revolts, but with his being as well !

That which he denies, even while he prophesies, he portrays, he *is*, himself : civilisation. All that belongs to it, all that it consists in : intellectualism, rationalism, relativism, cult of causality, of the "natural law"—with all that his theory is saturated ; and against that leaden historical materialism the materialism of a Marx is sheer blue-sky idealism. It is all pure nineteenth century, utterly *vieux jeu*, bourgeois through and through. It writes "civilisation" on the wall, as a revelation of what is to come ; but all the while itself is but civilisation's swan-song and dying echo.

The author has borrowed from Goethe the conception of morphology, but in his hands the idea developed—just as did in Darwin's the idea of evolution, likewise Goethe's. From Nietzsche he learned how to write, how to invest his words with the accents of fate. But his false and loveless austerity learned not a whit from him whose message was as unspeakably new as his spirit was sternly loving. He is a foe to spirit—not in the sense of culture but in that of the materialistic civilisation whose kingdom is of yesterday and not to-morrow. He is its true son, its latest master; inexorably and pessimistically prophesying its coming, while at the same time showing himself a secret conservative and a member of the party of culture.

In a word, he is a snob; and shows himself such in his attachment to nature, the natural law, and his contempt for spirit. "Might not the unchangeable laws of nature be a deception, and highly unnatural?" Novalis asks. "Everything acts according to law, and nothing acts according to law. Laws are simple, easily seen relations; we seek them for the sake of convenience." Yes, forsooth, for the sake of scientific convenience, and in sheer dictatorial lovelessness. And out of a self-complacency that lusts to betray its kind, that sides with nature against spirit and man, in nature's name arrogantly lays down the law to spirit and thinks itself monstrously elevated and irreproachable the while. But the problem of aristocracy, comprised of course in the conflict between nature and spirit, is not to be resolved by any such renegade attitude as this; and he who seeks, as does Spengler, to represent nature against spirit, must belong to the aristocracy of nature—like Goethe, who stood for it against Schiller's aristocracy of the spirit. Otherwise he is simply that which I just called the talented author of the *Decline*: namely, a snob, and a member of the very large class of modern personalities who uncomfortably indoctrinate views which they are unsuited to hold.

JOSEPH CONRAD'S "THE SECRET AGENT"

JOSEPH CONRAD'S "THE SECRET AGENT"

(*Preface to the German edition*)

ONCE before I have had occasion to write of a case like the present one : when I contributed a preface to an edition of *Peter Schlemil*, the happiest creation of a German writer of French nationality, and one of the best prized and loved of German literary possessions. And here, in this Polish Englishman, we have the modern pendant to Chamisso, only that this time we are translators only, it is not our national charms that are being flattered ! Yet that should not lessen our pleasure in the rare and beautiful phenomenon ; rather we should yield to its spell with enjoyment unmixed with envy—just as once others looked upon the phenomenon of Chamisso's German authorship. Cases of individuals of one nation falling in love with the life forms of another one ; of deliberate and definite emigration, complete personal and intellectual naturalisation into another sphere, as though nature had made a mistake and human intelligence had corrected it—such cases, it would seem, recur with a certain regularity in the history of culture, in the history of literature. And those whose healthy reverence for the natural is mingled with some little ironic doubt—probably less healthy but, humanly speaking, not without dignity—on the score of that undubitably holy element, will not be moved to sneer at the phenomenon as a monstrosity. On the contrary, they will note with sympathy and satisfaction a case of freedom from national limitations which did not issue in formlessness and mental death but in a universally admired cultural achievement.

It would be hard to say on what grounds to-day a Frenchman would make Germany his spiritual home. Once, in a more romantic time, it could happen out of love of poetry. We were the land of poets and thinkers ; to be a poet and to write German verse were, up to a point, one and the same thing. Who felt drawn to poesy felt drawn to Germany—Chamisso became German in order to be a German poet. But Conrad's case is different in kind ; not only the nations are different but also the times have changed. The Pole certainly did not become English in order to be an English writer. So far as I can learn, the idea was far from him. He became English to be a sailor—out of irresistible love of the sea. And here the two cases display likeness again : to be a sailor, Conrad might have become "a Russian, a Frenchman or a Prussian," he might have entered any of these marines, and thus it must have been that England and seafaring fell together, in the same way as once Germany and poetry to the author of *Peter Schlemil*. In both cases we have a shift of nationality caused by a passion for the main preoccupation of another people, the calling in which that one proverbially shines in the others' eyes. It was an accident of the time that Conrad's motive was in its nature less intellectual than Chamisso's.

But, after all, it would be rather old-fashioned and romantic to define the intellectual so narrowly as to make it synonymous with the literary. The Pole's love of the sea, which to him was the English thing, must always have been bound up with a deep sympathy for the essentially English, the English temperament and attitude toward life, the English accent and the spirit of its language ; such a passion is not possible to conceive without intellectual and speech elements. At bottom Conrad's conversion was scarcely less "poetic" than Chamisso's. And—after becoming an English sailor—he would scarcely have become an English author, had not creation been a primal impulse of his being ; if his whole strange course, away from all natural ties and into a foreign sphere of his own mysterious election, had not already been that of a dreamer and poet.

His love of the sea, of adventures at sea, was certainly a poet-love ; of her, of life upon her and with her, of that almost alone, he has written, even after he left her for the solid ground ; written in English, the classical tongue of the seafaring man—such English that, to a foreigner at least, it seems it could hardly be more so, and that to-day his

European reputation is that of a great British author.

When some years ago I visited The Hague, John Galsworthy was lecturing there on "Conrad and Tolstoi." Who it was, whom Galsworthy was setting beside the Russian colossus, I had no notion; and my amazement increased when I heard that André Gide had learned English in order to read Conrad in the original. Since that time I have read some of the best works by this narrative genius: the dæmonic story of a storm, called *The Nigger of the Narcissus*, and that of a calm, called *The Shadow Line*, also some of those whose scene is laid partly or wholly on shore, like *Chance*, a performance of great technical intricacy and brilliant virtuosity, and the altogether thrilling "crime story," *The Secret Agent*. I have read enough to feel it laid upon me to give something of him to the German public, whether maritime or not—and perhaps not maritime, perhaps just this very admirable *Secret Agent*, for the reason that it would be a limitation of Conrad's fame to speak of him only as a writer of sea-tales. I agree that this man's very deepest and most personal experience has been the sea, his perilous fellowship with that mighty element; certainly his greatest creative achievements lie in this field. But his virile talent, his Englishness, his free brow, his clear, steady and humorous eye, his narrative verve, power and grave-faced whimsicality, show up as well when the author stops on dry ground and observes what goes on there; sees it, sees through it and gives it form and body, as in the story lying before me, this exciting, yes, thrilling tale, a "crime story," as I said, and a political novel to boot, the history of a foreign embassy intrigue and its tragic human outcome.

It is an anti-Russian story, plainly enough, anti-Russian in a very British sense and spirit. Its background consists in politics on the large scale, in the whole conflict between the British and the Russian political ideology; I think it possible that this conflict has always formed the background—I will not say the motive—of the Pole's passionate love of England. If I were dealing with a German the hypothesis would be a doubtful one. We are metaphysicians; neither consciously nor unconsciously would we ever yield the political that much influence upon our mental life. But we have begun to feel that perhaps other people are different; and that feeling is the source of my guess that Polish Russophobia is here expressing itself in British.

And particularly in the figure of Mr. Vladimir, secretary to the representative of a foreign, all too foreign, power in London. The guilt of the whole affair lies at his door. He is a man of considerable elegance, though the author seems to agree with the verdict of one of the characters who calls him a "hyperborean swine." Of polished manners in general, he betrays in emotion a "somewhat oriental phraseology" and a guttural accent that is not only un-English but un-European, even Central Asiatic. "Descended from generations victimised by the instruments of arbitrary power," it says of him, "he was racially, nationally and individually afraid of the police. He was born to it. But that sentiment, which resembled the unnatural horror some people have of cats, did not stand in the way of his immense contempt for the English police." "The vigilance of the police," says he, or one of his subordinates says it for him, "and the severity of the magistrates! The general leniency of the judicial procedure here, and the utter absence of all repressive measures, are a scandal to Europe. What is wished for just now is the accentuation of the unrest—of the fermentation which undoubtedly exists." An international conference, that is, is to be held in Milan to combat social revolution. "What we want is to administer a tonic to the conference in Milan," he said airily. "Its deliberations upon international action for the suppression of political crime don't seem to get anywhere. England lags. This country is absurd with its sentimental regard for individual liberty. . . . England must be brought into line."

This anti-Sarmatic satire, however light the touch, speaks pride of English freedom and English civilisation in every line. Hated Russia, hated now in British but perhaps originally in Polish, is made to bear the guilt of all the human tragedy which is the matter of the novel: the death of little Stevie, the murder of the pitiable rascal Verloc and the suicide of his wife. Is Conrad more English in any of his shipboard tales than in this political detective story? An upright British Police Commissioner says to Mr. Vladimir: "What pleased me most in this affair, is that it makes such an excellent starting-point for a piece of work which I've felt must be taken in hand—that is, the clearing out of this country of all the foreign political spies, police, and that sort of—of—dogs." "Dogs" is an expression of Mr. Vladimir, an Oriental, Central-Asian sort of expression, to speak in that singular guttural tone which the Soviet agents of to-day probably command quite as well as did persons of Mr. Vladimir's kidney. I mention this only to show that our novel is not out of date because its action takes place under the Czars, and that the conflict of West and East which forms its political background has lost nothing in timeliness by a change of government.

And here another guess: the unequivocal, the even tendencious Western bias of this extraordinary writer, who has for years been famous in England, France and America—might it not perhaps be responsible for the limited scope of his reputation in a country like ours, which must always instinctively shrink from casting a decisive vote on one side or the other? There was a time when it looked as though we had chosen, as though we had voted, politically and culturally, on the side of the East; and that was just the time when Conrad's name was becoming celebrated throughout the Western world. For us the possessor of this narrative gift stands in the shadow of Dostoiewsky—a shadow which, we are free to confess, even to-day, we feel could swallow up three or four Conrads. And yet time changes all things; that epileptic, apocalyptic visionary has to a certain extent lost his power over the German mind; we are groping our way back from the Byzantine-Christian East to the Centre, and so to that in us which is of the humanistic and liberal West. Probably the very fact that a leading publisher is now getting out a German edition of Conrad's chief works is evidence of his better chances of success among us.

No, Conrad is far from being the size of Dostoiewsky. But is it size alone that conditions our love? If so, then our present epoch, which so far has produced forms much more slender and inconsiderable than those of the nineteenth century, would have small claims on our affections—and we have already pronounced on the latter as great indeed, though most unhappy. Let us confess that the products of our own century, so much less heroic than those of the nineteenth, do not even excel them in refinement. In Wagner, in Dostoiewsky, even in Bismarck, the nineteenth century combines a giant growth with the extreme of subtlety, with a refinement of technique which even borders on the morbid and the barbaric. But perhaps the very abandonment of this characteristic, at once sickly and savage, an Asiatic element, one might almost say, has actually conditioned the smaller structure of our own time. At least we do find it a more congenial and brotherly epoch, by contrast with the paternalistic spirit of yesterday. Perhaps our more modest scale is due to our aspirations toward a purer, brighter, healthier, almost might one say a more Greek humanity than the monumental gloom of the nineteenth century knew. And the Anglomania of Conrad the Slav, his scorn of Central Asian gutturals, may be rooted in these very aspirations—or this very task—of ours.

I would not forget the world-revolution, nor the spiritual advantages that to-day are bound up with good relations with the East. Every open-eyed Westerner to-day envies the Central European on purely geographical grounds, for advantages which would doubtless have to be surrendered in going over completely to the bourgeois West. In a sense we should have to reckon with a penalty—even without conceding that English against Continental-European means in itself a lowering of the level. More form, with more limitations—was that the alternative the Slav faced when he made his choice? No, that puts it badly. What he gave up were the advantages of barbarism, which he did open-eyed. What he got was reason, moderation, the open-minded attitude, intellectual freedom, and a humour that is saved by its Anglo-Saxon robustness from falling into the sentimental and bourgeois. A crisp, breezy humour it is, animated to some extent by the sentiment expressed somewhere in *The Secret*

Agent, that "this world of ours is not such a very serious affair after all." He shows small memory of the reverence for suffering that is a feature of Eastern Christianity; when he speaks of the hook which a poor old coachman has sticking out of his sleeve instead of an arm, he does so with a dryness that expresses grim enjoyment of life rather than a sense of pity. Often, in unobtrusive details, this humour is refreshingly comic: as when he describes the cab drive and the glass of the nearby-house fronts rattling and jingling as though about to collapse behind the cab; or the mechanical piano, whose keys seem to be played on by a vulgar and impudent ghost, who breaks off as though gone grumpy. The author does not, even faintly, change his key in describing a murdered man: "Mr. Verloc did not seem so much asleep now as lying down with a bent head and looking intently at his left breast. And when Comrade Ossipon had made out the handle of the knife he turned away from the glazed door and retched violently." Here all ado is lacking. The gaze turned upon the horrible is clear, lively, dry-eyed, almost gratified; the spirit of the narration is impressively English, and at the same time it is ultra-modern, post-middle-class. For I feel that, broadly and essentially, the striking feature of modern art is that it has ceased to recognise the categories of tragic and comic, or the dramatic classifications, tragedy and comedy. It sees life as tragi-comedy, with the result that the grotesque is its most genuine style—to the extent, indeed, that to-day that is the only guise in which the sublime may appear. For, if I may say so, the grotesque is the genuine anti-bourgeois style ; and however bourgeois Anglo-Saxondom may otherwise be or appear, it is a fact that in art the comic-grotesque has always been its strong point.

No, Conrad's leaning to the West is not an indication of artistic or intellectual surrender to the bourgeois point of view. He puts into Mr. Vladimir's mouth a question full of social and critical implications when he makes him ask : "I suppose you agree that the middle-classes are stupid ?" and when Mr. Verloc replies "They are," we have no doubt that the author shares the opinion of the two men. Conrad is too much artist and free spirit to be doctrinaire in his socialism—or to be Socialist at all save in the freest sense and as a child of his time. Marxism is represented in the book by the monomania of the solitary Michaelis, the "ticket-of-leave apostle." Conrad's revolutionaries are hardly lovable types ; the psychology of his social rebels is strongly pessimistic in kind ; and his scepticism of social utopias is revealed in the description of one insurgent of "an immense and nice hospital with a garden of flowers, in which the strong are to devote themselves to the nursing of the weak," whereas another, a miserable little terrorist and professor of dynamiting, dreams of quite another kind, a world like a slaughter-house, whither the "weak" are carried to be extinguished. But all this sarcasm is hardly bourgeois in intention. It is very pretty irony to say of the good Mr. Verloc that his function was to protect society, not to improve it or pass judgment upon it ; the irony becomes great satire when it deals with the main action of the book, the dynamite outrage which is to stimulate the Milan conference, and with the object upon which it would be most profitably directed. "Of course, there is art. A bomb in the National Gallery would make some noise. But it would not be serious enough. Art has never been the fetish of the middle-class. It's like breaking a few back windows in a man's house ; whereas if you want to make him really sit up, you must try at least to raise the roof. There would be some screaming, of course, but from whom ? Artists—art critics and such like, people of no account. . . . But there is learning—science. Any imbecile that has got an income believes in that. He does not know why, but he believes it matters somehow. It is the sacrosanct fetish. . . . It will alarm every selfishness of the class which should be impressed. They believe that in some mysterious way science is at the source of their material prosperity. They do. . . . Murder is always with us. It is almost an institution. The demonstration must be against learning—science. . . . What do you think of having a go at astronomy ? . . . There could be nothing better. . . . The whole civilised world has heard of Greenwich. The very bootblacks in the basement of

Charing Cross station know something of it. See? . . . Go for the first meridian. You don't know the middle-classes as well as I do. Their sensibilities are jaded. The first meridian. Nothing better, and nothing easier, I should think."

These judicious instructions of Mr. Vladimir to poor Verloc are the satirical height of the book. Its author is not, of course, the kind of creature who despises science. Nor, on the other hand, would he care much for a society based wholly upon it and throbbing to its dicta; and he speaks of "that glance of insufferable, hopelessly dense sufficiency which nothing but the frequentation of science can give to the dullness of common mortals." Disregard for art, for what constitutes the things of the mind, combined with boundless credulity and reverence for utilitarian science—that Conrad feels to be bourgeois. If his attitude toward the proletariat is not quite orthodox, that is obviously because science, on the other side of Marxism, has become the heritage and fetish of the proletariat; nobody will deny that Bolshevism is a sternly scientific conception of the world.

Comrade Ossipon, for instance—nicknamed "Doctor"; sometime medical practitioner without diploma, peripatetic lecturer to labour unions on the social future of hygiene, author of a confiscated pamphlet on "The Corroding Vices of the Middle Classes"—Comrade Ossipon is scientific. "Typical of this form of degeneracy" is what he says, condescendingly, of little Stevie's circle-drawing, that singular occupation, practised with so much assiduity, a cosmic chaos as it were, or the efforts of an insane art to portray the inconceivable. Of course Comrade Ossipon refers to the ear-lobes and to Lombroso. And "Lombroso is an ass," answers him a still greater enemy of the existing order ; and the author characterises this as a "shattering blasphemy." "Did you ever see such an idiot ? For him the criminal is the prisoner. Simple, is it not ? What about those who shut him up there—forced him in there ? . . . And what is crime ? Does he know that, this imbecile who has made his way in this world of gorged fools by looking at the ears and teeth of a lot of poor, luckless devils ? Teeth and ears mark the criminal ? Do they ? And what about the law that marks him still better—the pretty branding iron invented by the overfed to protect themselves against the hungry ? Red-hot applications on their vile skins, hey ? Can't you smell and hear from here the thick hide of the people burn and sizzle ? That's how criminals are made for your Lombrosos to write their silly stuff about." With all this "blasphemy" the author probably feels a certain, perhaps considerable, degree of sympathy. But his own way of looking at and describing little Stevie shows that his objections to Lombroso's science—as a cheapish middle-class product—rest not upon social grounds, but upon profounder, religious ones.

Stevie, as revealed during the cab-drive and the

ensuing conversation with his sister Winnie, in so far as his "peculiarity" permits one to speak of conversation; this deficient little Stevie, who nevertheless is lovable above and beyond all values in life, and whom Winnie so loves that she avenges his death in the most frightful, self-immolating manner —Stevie is far and away the finest figure in the book, and conceived with the liveliest and most affecting sympathy. Here Russian influence is plain: without Dostoiewsky's Idiot Stevie is unthinkable; we must admit that Dostoiewsky's attempt to present the purest and holiest in our humanity on a basis of the pathological is incomparably greater in its scope; yet here too we have an effort to canonise the clinically deficient. Our author's very modern power of seeing both sides is shown in his never belittling the pathological side of the case or romantically closing his eyes to it. He makes a naturalistic concession to science by characterising Stevie's "peculiarity" as a family trait; and gives pathological significance to his sister's deed by mentioning the sudden and striking likeness she shows with her brother at the moment of it. None the less, the dominant psychology here is one with a religious implication which shows Comrade Ossipon's "scientific" opinion of Stevie for what, from the human point of view, it really is: a shabby pseudo-education. Indeed, there is a subtle yet unmistakable suggestion that Comrade Ossipon's remark is what drops into the harassed mind of Verloc the first germ of the idea that he might use Stevie in the political crime he meditates ; thus science is once more compromised, once more found guilty from the human point of view.

All which is not bourgeois, but neither is it good orthodox proletarianism. It is evidence of the untrammelled objectivity which is the business of the class-free writer—if perhaps only his ; and everywhere in Conrad's books it is displayed at its liberating task. In his judgment of the sexes he is objective : speaks of the sensitivity that can exist in the masculine nature alongside exasperating brutality ; and finds that women are naturally more artful than men and much more ruthlessly avid for detail. So also he is aloof and critical in his attitude toward classes and masses, to all the apparent and temporary contradictions in the world. The sarcasm he directs against "hygienic idleness" as a form of existence is quite good socialism ; but he also knows how to make repulsive to the soul of the reader the type of the hoarse-voiced agitator—as in *The Nigger of the Narcissus* ; and he says of his terrorists that they are not a hair better than the powers invoked against them. "Like to like. The terrorists and the policemen both come from the same basket. Revolution, legality—counter moves in the same game." That is not the idle indifference of a detached observer. It is the refusal of a very much engaged intelligence to hang miserably in the air between contraries. "You revolutionists," he says, or makes someone

COSMOPOLITANISM

I HAVE sometimes been questioned upon my attitude toward cosmopolitanism; and always I have found the questions embarrassing. For I am, personally, no cosmopolite, no man of the world, anything but polyglot. I am no good to send abroad to represent my country; where German is not spoken—as in Holland, Hungary, Scandinavia—I am lost. My English, French and Italian are simply pathetic. Not only do I speak them like a schoolboy, I read them with difficulty. My indolence in respect to foreign languages was always unconquerable; and when I heard that André Gide learned English in order to be able to read Conrad in the original, my admiration, and my shame, knew no bounds. It was a painful moment when I had to confess to Galsworthy that I was still supinely awaiting a German version of the Polish sailorman's writings, as also a German version of Proust—make haste, ye international-minded German publishers!—and all my life I have been a rough-and-ready exploiter of the industry of German translators. I like to recall that it was a French novel, *Renée Mauperin*, by the brothers Goncourt, which in my young days, after repeated readings emboldened me to embark (I had already tried my hand at short-story writing) on a novel—*Buddenbrooks*. The Reclam version of *Renée Mauperin* began thus: " 'Do you not like society, Fräulein?' 'No, Sir, what would you, it bores me.' " I shall never understand how it is that my style was not utterly ruined by all the translations which I read in my youth.

On the best possible construction, my position toward "Europe" is rather like that of the eighteenth century, or of certain founders of German classicism, toward antiquity. Frederick the Great read the classics in French, which is no better than to read Balzac in German; and Schiller knew no Greek. Well, there are degrees and degrees of linguistic inadequacy; nobody is absolutely adequate. Who knows Hungarian? Yet we ought to be able to read Petofi in the original, and our own contemporary, Andreas Ady too, so passionately beloved in his own country. We western Europeans have most of us to put up with translations of the *Brothers Karamazov* and *Anna Karenina*; and Pushkin, who according to all Russians resembles Goethe—him we have just to do without. Yes, and how many of us, English, French or German, are capable of *Don Quixote* in the original? Fortunately for us Germans, our language is a flexible medium; it can take on the impress of a foreign idiom to a degree that enables a translation to reproduce the linguistic atmosphere of its original.

But, frankly, I must be head over ears in love with a work in a foreign tongue before I feel drawn to master it in the original. Certain passages from Shakespeare I have made my own; and Byron's *Don Juan*; and Claudel's *Annonce fait à Marie*. And I know by heart two or three of Verlaine's poems, in the dream-like, penetrating simplicity of their original French, for of course they exist in no other medium. All which does not alter the fact that in this respect I am no better and no worse than any average German who worshipped *Niels Lyne* when he was young, and has the *Insel* edition of Balsac on his shelves.

But—and it is up to this point that all my compromising admissions have been leading—is it a fact that the cosmopolitan spirit reaches us Germans only from without? By no means. And indeed, my national-minded friends, if we were hermetically to seal our frontiers on all four points of the compass and meet under Wotan's oak to vow, 'mid savage maledictions, that never again would we read a syllable of European literature, either in the original or translated; despite all we could do, that ideal of ethnic obscurantism would remain a wish-dream emanating from our own clouded brains. The enemy is in our midst. Goethe, Lichtenberg, Schopenhauer—there is no help for it, these are European prose, in the original German. And there were also a couple of domestic events, from whose influence no German who was young round the turn of the century could possibly insulate himself, and which were even more shattering to the domestic idyll. I mean Nietzsche and Wagner. I have already been driven to say some good things on this subject before now.

The whole writing tribe is in a bad, a ridiculous position. We forget what we have said, once we have said it. We get rid of our ideas by giving them form and sending them on their travels. After that they live in time and belong to others more than to ourselves. I early made the discovery that giving a thing literary expression is a little like killing it. It deals the quietus, interest is dead. A writer gets progressively duller by making others wiser. He may even, after that, thank other people for telling him something which he said himself first.

I have been reading an essay by a Viennese writer named Leszer, in that friendly and excellently edited Swiss review, *Wissen und Leben*. The essay is entitled "New Narrative Prose," and it has things in it that please me a good deal—because they are by me. Or, rather, in the days of my devastating cleverness they were by me. Now they are by Leszer—and most instructive I find them. Leszer refers to the Europeanisation of German prose by Nietzsche. The genealogist of morals, according to Leszer, could have counted on the fingers of one hand all the existing German works that were up to the standard of European prose. But since 1900 things have changed for the better: German narrative art has produced not a few works on a high, and some on the highest, plane, both linguistically and intellectually speaking. Nietzsche's mission, says Leszer, has pre-eminently been "to turn the intellectual German into one still more intellectual; with the result that the artistic and the intellectual have flowed together, and German literature, bent on hewing to the line, on dialectical tension and antithetical refinements, has continued to gain in intellectual pace. This spectacle of the transformation of the German as a human being and, as a necessary consequence, the transformation of German literature, has frequently a bewildering effect, as can daily be seen; it produces some very cutting literary criticism, especially from those narrow-minded conservatives who wear their heads turned the wrong way and are for conceding full marks for literary and creative excellence only to dyed-in-the-wool products of the German temperament, good and dull and yearning, ingenuous and long-drawn-out. Obstinately set as they are against the inevitable restratification of the German world, they make their own pseudo-sensitive and invincibly stupid valuations and bear witness to their utter poverty of counsel for the future." Severe, but not unjust. Lord, but he knows how to give it to the creatures! He speaks of Flake (whose influence is strongly educative in its nature), and praises the Alsatian writer for his profound "love of form, of the ordered and perspicuous, of dry air and a bright sky"—for qualities, in short, which one might almost call

Latin, save that by dint of such spirits as my brother and myself they are gradually becoming German. "Gradually becoming German!" So that too can come to pass! Something that was not German can actually become so, and thus no longer fall under the reproach of being un-German? It belongs, then, to the nature of cosmopolitanism that the character of a people is not rigidly, unchangeably fixed and definite, but malleable, susceptible of training and development? Yes, it seems that there are encounters, interpenetrations of the individual and the national. A writer can become more German, while simultaneously changing the face of his nation in the eyes of the world. Perhaps one ought not to disturb such profound and delicate changes by talking about them. But one may just possibly draw the conclusion that the cosmopolitan spirit is something else than skill in languages and world-dilettantism. But what, then, is the cosmopolitan spirit? Perhaps nothing but the spirit of life and change.

Another interesting fact: an Italian with the barbaric name of Suckert, a Fascist theorist, has in a book called *Living Europe* presented a psychology of the hero which may give offence to many, and even so be quite worth talking about. Heroes, Suckert says, are *not* representative personages; they are not the embodiment of a nation's faults and virtues, but precisely the people who show variations from these. Therein lies their peculiarity "Heroes are the negative expression of a nation, the exception not the rule, deviation from, not conformity with, the race whence they spring. The office of representing the people falls not to the geniuses but to the mediocrities. Vincenzo Monti is more Italian than Dante or Leopardi, Boileau more French than Pascal or Descartes. The geniuses are the expression of what the people is not." Pretty insulting, isn't it? We are mediocre in so far as we are representative, in so far as we are national. We are heroic only in so far as we are strangers among our own, and compel our own to things that they have no mind to. Well, anyhow, the "in so far" is consoling. A dash of mediocrity is permissible, might even be necessary. Bismarck, for instance, was very odd in some ways, and certainly he drove his Germans into courses at which they must have shuddered in their souls. But he would scarcely have been able to do it had he not also been very German of very German—a perfect explosion of the essential characteristics of his race. And to return to the literary and cultural sphere: Goethe himself, at the time of the war of liberation, had his "Germanicity" enthusiastically vouched for by such spokesmen as Jahn and Varnhagen. Ernst Bertram has lately published a fine analysis of irrational and metaphysical characteristics in Lichtenberg; and I remember myself calling attention to the German element in Schopenhauer's European prose, in particular to his language chauvinism. In short, a little mediocrity is strengthening to the faith. It makes possible things that were otherwise not so. Your Mussolini, *caro* Suckert, is, you will admit, Italian enough. Then let us too be a little genuine, a little traditional, domestic and German. It might, under some circumstances, be but one temptation the more towards cosmopolitanism.

The "mediocre," in other words, the Germanic master-craftsman element was overwhelming in Wagner. Here the temptation almost assumes the character of a deliberate trick. Yes, a whole people can be led by the hero appointed to transform them, once he is disguised as a *Meister*. To think that to-day Wagner—whom aforetime European artists and decadents like Baudelaire were the earliest to acclaim—can be invoked in the revivals at Bayreuth as the patron saint of the obscurantist spirits of Germany, the representative of rude virtue! Nietzsche made extravagant fun of the misunderstandings Wagner gave rise to amongst us Germans: reading it was the keenest critical experience of my life.

The whole endlessly fascinating Wagner case itself shows the rôle which the German spirit—accustomed as one is to think of it as simple, pious and conservative—has already on occasion played in the world: the rôle, I mean, of a destructive force, of sinister Europeanism. This is the subject—not quite mastered, perhaps, yet enormously interesting—of Franz Werfel's *Verdi*. Leszer, my informant, says as much in the Swiss article on which my remarks are based. "The contrast," he writes, "between the sacred old-Italian folk-music of Verdi and the metaphysical, dialectical, intellectual subtlety of Wagner's; the deep gulf fixed between the two men: Verdi with his shrinking shyness and pure objectivity, Wagner with his lust of the world and reprehensible thirst for triumph." I read all that with a sympathy bordering on passion. "Metaphysical, dialectical music"—it could not be better put. But did Wagner ever play in Germany any other rôle than just the one he played in Italy, where the old *Meister* and pied piper lured the youth of the nation away from Verdi into his intellectualistic-European enchanted mountain? Despite that too, too German soul of his, that sent the water to his blue, blue eyes, was his mission amongst us ever anything but that same cosmopolitan disintegration and change, that "turns the intellectual German of yesterday into a still more intellectual one"? An historical question, this; as also in its way a matter of conscience. But one must not linger too long over such; each must be, and each keep to his destiny. Freedom from scruple is a condition of productivity; and to myself and others I have often said that in national as in cosmopolitan matters everything depends on being and doing, and as good as nothing on saying and thinking.

But the question I have been asked was a personal one. What do I, individually, owe to the cosmopolitan spirit ? I reply that my happiest and most fruitful encounters with it were inside our own borders ; that I came into touch with cosmopolitanism, Europeanism, primarily in German, and that my contacts were called Goethe, Lichtenberg, Schopenhauer, Nietzsche and Wagner. The last two, earliest in point of time, were also, the one critically, the other in a general artistic sense, the most powerful and decisive. The critical was the more ethical, as it were the more respectable ; the artistic was suspect, equivocal, yet infinitely full of magic and stimulation. All that I know of good and of triumph over self I owe to the one. All of evil and temptation to the other. And yet to both, to the evil not less than to the good, I owe it that a French critic can speak of the "*lucidité critique de sa pensée qui est celle d'un moraliste européen.*"

ON THE FILM

ON THE FILM

I SOMETIMES allow my thoughts to dwell on the film—one day I shall be uttering them at length. But just now all I can say is, that lately I have come to entertain feelings for this phenomenon of our time that amount to a lively interest, even almost to a passion. I go often to the cinema ; for hours on end I do not tire of the joys of spectacle spiced with music ; whether it be travel pictures, scenes from the wild, the weekly news of the world, a diverting piece of tomfoolery, a "thriller" or a "shocker," or a touching tale of love. The actors must be good to look at, with a gift of expression, vain if you like but never unnatural ; the "story" itself may be vastly silly, provided—as is nearly always the case to-day—the silliness or sentimentality is set in a frame of scenic and mimic detail which is true to life and to reality, so that the human triumphs persistently over the crude falsity of the performance as a whole.

I used the word phenomenon above—and advisedly, since in my view the film has little to do with art, and I would not therefore approach it with criteria drawn from the artistic sphere, as do certain humanistic-minded and conservative souls, who then in sorrow and contempt turn away their eyes from the offending spectacle as from a base-born and inordinately democratic form of mass entertainment. For me, I despise it myself—but I love it too. It is not art, it is life, it is actuality. Compared with art's intellectual appeal its own is crudely sensational; it is the same as that of life itself upon a passive onlooker, who at the same time is aware that he himself is pretty comfortable and that what he sees is "nothing but a play." At the same time his sensations are heightened by the accompanying music. But now tell me: why is it people weep so, at the cinema? Or, rather, why do they fairly howl, like a maidservant on her afternoon out? We all went to the first performance of *The Big Parade* and met Olaf Gulbransson at the exit. That jolly and muscular Eskimo was drowned in tears. "I haven't wiped my face yet," said he by way of excuse: we stood there together for a while, quite simply, unaffectedly, with streaming eyes. Is that the mood in which one turns away from a work of art, leaves a picture, puts down a finished book? It is true, elderly gentlemen do shed tears, at *Alt Heidelberg*, when they hear "*O alte Burschenherrlichkeit*"; but even elderly gentlemen do not weep over Shakespeare, or Kleist, or Gerhard Hauptmann. Say what you like, the atmosphere of art is cool; it is a sphere of spiritual valuations, of transmuted values; a world of style, a manuscript world, objectively, in the most personal sense, preoccupied with form; a sphere of the understanding

—"*denn sie kommt aus dem Verstande*," says Goethe. It is chaste and elegant, it is significant, it is serene; its agitations are kept sternly at second hand; you are at court, you control yourself. But take a pair of lovers on the screen, two young folk as pretty as pictures, bidding each other an eternal farewell in a real garden, with the grass waving in the wind—to the accompaniment of the meltingest of music; and who could resist them, who would not blissfully let flow the tear that wells to the eye? For it is all raw material, it has not been transmuted, it is life at first hand; it is warm and heartfelt, it affects one like onions or sneezewort. I feel a tear trickling down in the darkness, and in silence, with dignity, I rub it into my cheekbone with my finger-tip.

And the film has, quite specifically, nothing to do with the drama. It is narrative in pictures. That these faces are present to your sight does not prevent their greatest effectiveness from being in its nature epic; and in this sphere, if in any, the film approaches literary art. It is much too genuine to be theatre. The stage setting is based upon delusion, the scenery of the film is nature itself, just as the fancy stimulated by the story creates it for the reader. Nor have the protagonists in a film the bodily presence and actuality of the human figures in the drama. They are living shadows. They speak not, they are not, they merely *were*—and were precisely as you see them—and that is narrative. The film possesses a technique of recollection, of psychological suggestion, a mastery of detail in men and in things, from which the novelist, though scarcely the dramatist, might learn much. That the Russians, who have never been great dramatists, are supreme in this field, rests, without any doubt in my mind, upon their narrative skill.

As an author I have not as yet had much luck with the films. *Buddenbrooks* has been filmed, but hardly to the satisfaction of the friends of that book. Instead of narrating, only narrating, and letting the characters speak for themselves, what has been made of it is a poorish play of merchant life, in which not much remains of the book save the names. A very good Berlin producer did think for a while of filming *The Magic Mountain* ; which is not surprising, for a bold treatment of it might have produced a wonderful spectacle, a fantastic cyclopædia, with a hundred digressions into all points of the compass : visions of all the worlds of nature, sport, research, medicine, politics, all grouped round an epic core. What might not have been made simply of the chapter "Snow," with its Mediterranean dream poem of humanity ! But it is not to be. Such a production made too great material and intellectual demands. *Royal Highness* is under consideration. It is simple and should succeed ; there are good rôles, including that always irresistible one of a good dog ; and though the subject-matter might be reminiscent of *Alt Heidelberg*, with good settings and well-chosen actors it should be a pleasing piece and very likely a successful one.

SLEEP, SWEET SLEEP

SLEEP, SWEET SLEEP

THAT daily the night falls ; that over stresses and torments, cares and sorrows the blessing of sleep unfolds, stilling and quenching them ; that ever anew this draught of refreshment and lethe is offered to our parching lips, ever after the battle this mildness laves our shaking limbs ; that from it, purified from sweat and dust and blood, strengthened, renewed, rejuvenated, almost innocent once more, almost with pristine courage and zeal we may go forth again— these I hold to be the benignest, the most moving of all the great facts of life. Creatures of blind urge we step out of the tranquil night to roam the day. The sun burns us, we tread upon thorns and flints, our feet bleed, our breath comes panting. What horror were the burning road we trudge to stretch before us to the horizon's edge, unbroken, without nearer goal ! Who would have strength to follow it to the end, who would not sink down in rue and bitterness ? But familiar night slips in between again, and yet again, upon the road of our passion ; each day has its goal ; a green twilight, a murmuring spring, a grove awaits us, where soft moss consoles our feet, our brows are cooled with blissful airs of home and peace ; and with arms outstretched, head dropping backward, with opening lips, with eyes grown blessedly dim, we enter within its priceless shades.

They tell me that I was a quiet child, that I did not cry and break the peace, but was given to sleep and dreams, to a degree most comfortable to my nurses. I believe it ; for I remember loving sleep and forgetfulness at a time when I had hardly anything to forget ; and well I know what it was that made the indelible impression upon my mind and fanned my latent fondness to a conscious love. It was the tale of the man who did not sleep ; who was so abandonedly committed to time and affairs that he invoked a curse on sleep, and an angel granted him the awful boon of sleeplessness, breathing on his eyes till they became like grey stones in their sockets, and their lids never closed again. How this man came to rue his wish ; what he had to bear as a sleepless solitary among men, dragging out his doomed and tragic life, until at last death released him, and night, that had stood inaccessible before his stony eyeballs, took him to and into herself ; such details I have forgotten, and only know that I could scarcely wait for the evening of that day to be left alone in my bed, to throw myself upon the bosom of slumber. And never have I slept more profoundly than in the night after I heard that story.

Since then I have read with pleasure all that has been written in books in praise of sleep : the theory, for instance, of Mesmer, to the effect that sleep, in which the life of plants consists and from which the infant in its first few weeks of life wakes only to be fed, may be perhaps the normal, original state of man, immediately corresponding to his vegetative needs. "May we not say," asks that gifted charlatan, "that we wake only to sleep again ?" An admirable idea. And the waking state is of course only a stage in the battle to regain the longed-for haven. Darwin supports us in the theory that our minds have developed as a weapon in the struggle for existence—a dangerous weapon indeed, which, when no outward peril threatens we too often turn upon ourselves. Well for us, then, when our weapon is sheathed, when the dazzling and consuming flame of consciousness slowly quenches upon the world about us and within us, and we may give ourselves once more to our true and happy state !

But even if it is necessity that sometimes rouses us from our slumber, yet it is not necessity that actually keeps us from it. Can you believe me when I say that the sleeplessness of worry or affliction is quite unknown to me ? It was only, I think, when the care-free days of early childhood were over and the ugliness of life, in the guise of school, began to deform my day, that I first slept with passion ; and never more blissfully than between certain Sunday nights and Monday mornings, when after a day of sheltered life, when I might belong to myself and my family, the next impended again, with harsh, unkindly toil. So it has been ever since : I never sleep more profoundly, never am more aware of a sweet home-coming to the bosom of the night, than when I am wretched, when my work goes badly, despair weighs me down and disgust of human kind frightens me into the darkness. And how else, I inquire, can it be, since care and pain could never strengthen our hold on day and time ?

You will smile to hear that I preserve a clear and grateful memory of every bed I ever slept in for any length of time : every single one, from the earliest little railed, green-curtained cot to the majestic mahogany resting-place in which, in fact, I first saw the light, and which for many years stood in my bachelor quarters. My present bed is less heavy : it is an English white-enamelled one, with open-work head and foot, and above it hangs in a white frame a French picture called the *Marche à l'étoile*, with a melting, swooning, mellifluous blue atmosphere—to me it is the finest decoration my alcove could possess. You will smile, I say—and yet : what high rank in the hierarchy of our household goods is held by the bed, metaphysical chattel that it is, wherein are celebrated the mysteries of birth and death ? It is a sweet-odoured linen shrine, where we lie unconscious, our knees drawn up as once in the darkness of the womb, attached anew, as it were, to nature's umbilical cord and by mysterious ways drawing in nourishment and renewal ; it is a magic cockle-shell, standing covered and unheeded by day in its corner, wherein by night we rock out upon the sea of forgetfulness and infinity.

Infinity . . . the sea . . . Old as my love of sleep is my love of the sea, whose vast simplicity I have always preferred to the exacting many-sidedness of mountain scenery. And these two loves have a common source. I have in me much of the Hindu, much heavy and sluggish craving after that form or no-form of consummation which is called Nirvana, or nothingness. Notwithstanding that I am an artist, I own to a most unartist-like bent toward the infinite, a dislike of measure and articulation. And the opposites to this, believe me, are discipline and training; they are—to use the sternest word I can find to express them—morality. What, then, is morality, and what the morality of the artist?

Morality has a double aspect. It must take as well as give, be capable of gathering up equally with giving out, for one without the other is never moral. The accumulative half of the process, the creative converse of giving out, of which Grillparzer makes his priest say such glorious things, must be felt to be understood; but to me its profoundest expression is, strange to say, the image of the fœtus as it grows in the womb. The human head, that is, is not round from the start, only needing to get larger. The face is open in front, it grows from both sides, slowly, slowly closing in to form this symmetrical, seeing, willing, individually concentrated countenance of ours, the expression of the ego. And this image, of a closing in and together, a shaping itself a form out of a world of possibilities, sometimes gives me an inkling of what is going on behind the phenomenon. I conceive that all individual existence is to be interpreted as a supra-sensual act of the will, a resolve to concentrate, limit and take shape, to assemble out of nothingness, to renounce freedom and infinity and all slumbering and weaving in spaceless and timeless night: an ethical resolve to be and to suffer. Yes, mere *becoming* is ethical—would not Christian theologians have it that our greatest sin consists in having been born? Only the Philistine considers that sin and morality are opposed ideas; they are one, for without knowledge of sin, without yielding to harm and destruction, all morality is nothing but sheer flabby virtuousness. It is not purity and innocence which are morally desirable, not cautious egoism and a contemptible knack at keeping a good conscience; not these, but the struggle and compulsion, the pain and passion, that make up morality. Heinrich von Kleist says somewhere: "Whoever loves life with too careful a love, that man is already dead, morally speaking; since the greatest strength of his life, the power to resign it, is rotting while he hugs it in his arms." And what say the Gospels? Their most ethical message is: "Resist not evil."

The morality of the artist consists in this "gathering," this power of egoistic concentration, this will to form, to limit, to shape, to embody; to give up the freedom of the infinite, the slumbering and weaving in the unbounded realms of the emotions. It is, in a word, the will to effectiveness. But all work born of an artist's cold, calculated and correct resolve is bad, ignoble, bloodless, repellent. His true morality lies in abandonment, devotion, in surrender and error; in struggle and compulsion, experience, knowledge, passion.

Morals are undoubtedly life's highest concern; perhaps they are even the very will to live. But if the saying that life is not the highest of goods is anything more than an empty phrase, then there must be something higher than this will. And precisely as morals function to correct and discipline the free possible into the limited and actual, so perhaps morals in their turn need a corrective, a ceaseless admonition, never quite to go unheeded, a call to withdrawal and communion. If this be wisdom, then its opposite will be the folly of the man who cursed sleep and clung with blind eagerness to time and day. If it be religious feeling, then its opposite will be the pagan animality that walks with its snout to the earth and sees not the great peace of the stars overhead. If it be the aristocratic position, then its opposite will be the coarseness that feels itself wholly at home in life and reality, knowing no yearning and no higher abode. There are, we all know, men so imperishably ordinary and hearty that one cannot imagine them dying, or ever partaking of the consecration of death.

It has significance for more than our nervous systems, this fact that what robs us of sleep is not depression but passion: what Gautama Buddha calls "clinging," the hot involvement of our ego with the hour and the act. It means that the soul has lost its home, has been carried so far away that it cannot find its way back. But it is precisely the men whose activities and passions are the greatest and strongest who seem most easily to find the way back. I have read that Napoleon could fall asleep at will, in the daytime, in the midst of a crowd, in the din of a swaying battle. The memory comes back to me of a painting—of no great value as a work of art, perhaps, but as anecdote I find it charming. It is called "*C'est lui*"; and shows a poor peasant room, with man, wife and children huddled at the open door and shyly peering in. And there, in the middle of the room, bolt upright on the table, sits the Emperor, and sleeps. He sits there, this personification of aggressive and egoistic passions; he has taken off his sword, his lax fist rests on the table, his chin is sunk on his breast, he sleeps. He needs no quiet, no pillow, no darkness, to forget the world; he sits on any hard seat to hand, shuts his eyes, leaves all behind—and sleeps.

Surely that man is the greatest who keeps faith with and yearns for the night, the while he performs the mightiest tasks of the day. And so it is that I love best that work which was born out of "yearning after the holy night," and as it were in despite of itself stands to-day glorious both in slumber and in strength of will—I mean Richard Wagner's *Tristan und Isolde*.